WHAT READERS ARE SAYING...

"Mary takes the subject of you as an individual and walks you through her personal journey while identifying tools of self-awareness in a practical format that anyone can use. *Your Story is a Circle* uses the analogy of drawing a circle around one's self, but if paying attention, I see her circle as a point of illumination from the center of self. A circle also containing your own light. It is for you but can be positively shared with others."

~ Richard Kathlean, Emmy-Nominated Executive Producer and Former Student of Mary K. Hild

"Along the way I have acquired many of the same Tools Mary describes. Several years ago, at a day-long retreat on Welcoming Prayer, a wonderful teacher used a phrase that I love: 'We hold a flashlight on the path for others.' Mary is holding a flashlight with her book as a guide that shines light on many healing insights available to us all."

~ Mary Kay Taylor, Counselor, Retired

"Mary writes with heartfelt candor about her personal journey of awakening. We walk with her from suffering to freedom, while never getting bogged down in victimhood. Her story is relatable and real, a guiding light that raises the frequency of both the reader and the planet!"

~ Kara McKay

"This book was reading my Story – everyone's Story. Leading to soul searching, revealing baggage we all carry and giving us tools on how to start the process of healing and forgiveness within ourselves."

~ Lynn Mathiason

"As a senior and a veteran who has experienced life in the same way this book describes, I have found that, male or female, we all have to find that person we are inside and accept ourself."

~ Ron McKay

Your Story is a Circle

MARY K. HILD, MED
Counselor, Teacher

Story Circle Press

Story Circle Press

Federal Way, Washington

ISBN number:
Print: 979-8-9852179-0-2

Cover Design: Mary K. Hild

Writing Coach and Editor: Micah (MJ) Schwader
www.inspiredlifepublications.com

Printed in the United States of America

DEDICATION

My dad, the love of my life. You are my muse, my inspiration. You gave me the courage to open up my heart, take down the shield, and allow love in. In life and death, you are always with me - inspiring, encouraging, loving. I am grateful and truly blessed to have you as my dad! Thank you!

I am grateful to God, Source Energy, Universe, Divine Life, Higher Power, Creator, for me, a soul, as a part of your Pure Love Energy. Your guiding light and love are always a part of me.

ACKNOWLEDGMENTS

To all the many lives that have touched mine. You've all inspired me to write this book by helping me grow in so many ways by sharing your gifts.

Spiritualists, uplifters, messengers, and guides who have inspired me, influenced me and contributed to this book:

Abraham-Hicks, Rhonda Byrne, Brene Brown, Pema Chodron, Deepak Chopra, Daily word by Unity, Joe Dispenza, Mike Dooley, Wayne Dyer, Thích Nhất Hạnh, David Hawkins, Louise Hay, Robert Holden, Dalai Lama, Sonja Lyubomirsky, Ainslie MacLeod, CJ (Connie Jo) Mortinson, Mary Morrissey, Caroline Myss, Michael Newton, Kelly Notaras, Nick Ortner, Osha, Marisa Peer, Cheryl Richardson, David Richo, don Miguel Ruiz, Janice Sack-Ory, Marci Schimoff, Helen Schucman (ACIM – A Course in Miracles), Florence Scovel Shinn, Amit Sood, Eckhart Tolle, Doreen Virtue, Neale Donald Walsch, Brian Weiss, Sara Wiseman.

CONTENTS

INTRODUCTION:
FROM DEPRESSION TO JOY

In this book, I will take you with me on my journey as a woman, a person, a teacher, a lover, a companion, and a friend as I discovered that I am more than a human being doing human things; I am a spiritual being doing soul things – just like you. In sharing my Story, I will show you that it is possible to change your life from just living to being joyfully alive. You'll learn simple skills that will help you find the real you and live happily ever after.

In the following pages, you're going to:

- Hear my Story, from my childhood misbeliefs, how they affected me in adulthood, and how that led to depression
- Discover you have a Story
- Learn why your Story is a Circle
- Understand the tools I used to overcome depression, find the real me, and love myself, resulting in being happy from the

inside out with the realization that I had it
inside myself, all along

By sharing my Story, I'll reveal some of the most
profound and most personal moments of my life. It's
not my intent to portray anyone, my mother, rela-
tives, spouse, or friends in a negative way. No one is
to blame. No one set out to hurt me. No one is at
fault; we are all human, and we each have our own
Story.

My Story is my perception and internalization of
events in my life and how I chose to act on those
events. These are my observations, feelings, and
interpretations. I own the way I perceived well-
meaning behaviors and words. Each individual in
my Story acted from their own Story, and I have the
utmost respect and love for them. Our experiences
together have made me who I am today.

All of my experiences, the good and the challenging, led me to take responsibility for my happiness.
Step-by-step, I did just that. It wasn't always easy,
but it was needed and ultimately rewarding. I've
created a toolbox from my experiences, and I call it

the Turn Me On (TMO) Toolbox. Later in the book, I'll show you how to create your own TMO Toolbox.

You and I are alike – and different. We live every day, eating, sleeping, working, parenting, playing, laughing, crying, interacting with others, and surviving. And yet, some of us live glamorous lives, some of us live ordinary lives, some of us have lives filled with struggle, some of us live comfortably, and all varieties of life in between. But no matter how different our lives are, in the end, we all have the same needs: attention, acceptance, appreciation, affection, and allowing. We'll learn more about these and how to attain them later in the book.

But no matter how different our lives are, in the end, we all have the same needs: attention, acceptance, appreciation, affection, and allowing.

My Story has a happy ending. I don't know how or where my physical life will progress, but I know that I will always grow, learn, and follow my inner and outer happiness to pure love and joy.

Looking at your Story can do the same for you. Dr. Amit Sood says, "In the physical domain, healing restores structure and function. Psychological healing restores hope, happiness, and fulfillment. Spiritual healing involves finding a deeper meaning for our suffering, and through that search, uncovering the meaning of life."

We are all on this journey to happiness and love. Sometimes it's a bumpy road, and sometimes the road is smooth and comfortable; it all depends on you. Eckhart Tolle said: "The primary cause of unhappiness is never the situation, but your thoughts about it."

How about you? Do you want to come along with me and take a look at your life and your journey? Life is worth living! We are here for a reason, and we are here for a purpose! Let's find our internal soul happiness together because we are the same. I deserve it! You deserve it! Let's go. Woohoo!!!

CHAPTER I

MY STORY, MY CIRCLE

Mary Kay: A soul, a body, and a mind that came into this world on September 14, 1953. Many years later, when I finally slowed my life down and took a close look inside, these are the questions I asked myself...

"Who Am I?"

"Am I a human being?"

"Am I a soul?"

"Why am I here? Why was I born?"

"What is my purpose? What did I come into this world to do?"

In the past, I would have answered those questions like this:

Who am I? – "I am a female, a 60-year-old woman who is tall, thin, Slovanian, a nice person, educated, and accomplished in my career and personal life. I am living my life like most everyone else, according to society's standards, and doing the best I can."

Am I a human being? – "I see myself mostly in a physical, human sense and not much beyond or deeper than that."

Am I a soul? – "I was raised to believe there is a God and I have a soul, but I have no clue what that means. I never give it much thought. I think when I die, I will go to Heaven, whatever that is, and be at peace."

Why am I here? Why was I born? – "I was born to go through life like everyone else, striving for the 'American Dream,' making money, working hard, living comfortably, enjoying life, having fun, raising children, and retiring to a life of leisure."

What is my purpose? What did I come into this world to do? – "I am a teacher and counselor, and my purpose is to be good at my chosen career path by making a positive difference in my student's lives. I am a caring person, friend, and wife to the people in my life."

What is clear by these answers is that I defined myself by what I did, how I looked, the people in my life, and what effect I had on them and they on me.

When depression forced me to slow my life down and go deep within, I looked back to my earliest memories to find why I was the way I was, what I did and why I did it, and what I thought and why I thought it. I pulled out all parts of my life, past and present, and laid them out in front of me to examine in more depth. This part of my journey – my Story – had me asking some uncomfortable questions and reliving painful memories. All the while, I knew I had to wade through depths of emotions to answer the questions that burned in me for answers.

How would you answer these questions? Take a moment and reflect on this because only you will ever know. What does it feel like to be you? Do you believe that you are loveable and good enough? When do you believe that you are loveable and good enough? What does loveable and good enough mean? What does it take to feel you are loved: Attention from others? Acknowledgment? Affection (hugs, kisses, words)? Appreciation? Acceptance? Spending time? Giving of time? Gifts? Sex? Party invitations? Making money?

Do you feel shame and guilt over an event or experience? Do you feel that something is your fault, and you blame yourself? Do you feel like you have to justify everything you do, say, or think? Do you want to take back control of your life? Do you want to stop listening to other people's beliefs and opinions? Do you want to love yourself? Do you want to be happy from the inside out?

These are the questions I asked to discover who I truly am and what I wanted for myself. My journey to acceptance that I am loveable and good enough evolved as I examined my inner self. I started from the misbelief that my needs would be met by others to ultimately learning that I could meet my needs myself.

My journey to acceptance that I am loveable and good enough evolved as I examined my inner self. I started from the misbelief that my needs would be met by others to ultimately learning that I could meet my needs myself.

We can't escape change. What we can do is find the best way to change and become what we desire. I desired to be happy from the inside out, and I knew that it was possible. It is possible for you, too, if you believe it and want it.

How will you know when you've found what you desire? When you feel it, you know it in your heart. You may have had moments throughout your life when you have felt it. I have. I want to feel that feeling all of the time, every moment, even when something sad is happening in my life. I want to be able to feel sad but not have the sadness consume me. What I want to be consumed with is a heart and soul full of happiness and love, despite what impacts me in life.

I want to be able to feel sad but not have the sadness consume me. What I want to be consumed with is a heart and soul full of happiness and love, despite what impacts me in life.

CHAPTER 2

YOUR STORY IS A CIRCLE OF LIFE, A CIRCLE OF LOVE

"All beginnings have ends and all ends have beginnings; it's a Circle." ~ Mary Hild

A Circle is a symbol representing the endlessness of existence. Everything flows; there is no past or present. There is only the now. There is no beginning, and there is no end.

In the same way, your soul's journey never ends – the unending cycle of birth, death, and rebirth make your Story a Circle. Your Circle is simply your soul transferring from one life form to another, going from spiritual to physical and back to spiritual again and again. Some have referred to this as reincarnation or incarnations, where the soul's learning, evolution, and journey continue unending. From this view of your soul's journey, every life you live fits together with all of your other lives.

Another way of looking at it is as if your life were a movie, a movie where you are the star. Every character in your movie, every person in your life, has a role to play. They were explicitly cast for the part you need each to play: husband, wife, mother, father, siblings, best friend, family, acquaintances, boss, etc. You created the storyline of your movie to learn some lessons; the cast is here to help you do that. Once your soul leaves your body and returns to the spiritual realm, it rests, regroups, and, when it's ready to, returns to a new body to continue learning and evolving, creating a new Story (making another movie).

I don't worry about making mistakes or having regrets in life because I will have a choice to come back. As peaceful as the spiritual realm is, I think I wouldn't want to stay there, stop growing, and no longer have new physical experiences and challenges. Why would I want to repeat high school if I'd already graduated? That would be boring in physical form and equally boring in non-physical spiritual form. My soul's energy needs the stimulation of learning new things.

However, when we are born, all our spiritual/soul memories are erased. Where we came from with all its happiness, peace, and love, all our past lives and who we were in them, all of our gifts, all our previous lessons learned and not learned, our soul families, souls we know, souls that guide us – everything about who we are is forgotten. It has to be for us to live our lives freely and experience life fully. All the ups and downs, pain, and sadness of this bumpy road of life on earth have to be experienced by us anew with no previous life memories.

The world we live in is our school. What would be the point of returning to earth and living if we knew all the answers in advance and there was nothing to learn or to offer to others? What would we strive for?

We come to create, learn, and to teach. We come to experience all that we can, and sometimes that is through heartache and pain. We come to give all that we can regardless of our resources. We come to help each other and pass on love and goodness. We come to strive to make this world a better place. We come to remember who we are.

Even so, not everyone can maintain the pure love from which we are born. As you experience all the influences in this world from culture, family, friends, schooling, religions, and media, your free will allows you to make choices about everything in your life – both good choices and bad choices. You can choose to be a good and compassionate person or choose to be a hurtful and evil person. You make these choices every day based on your situation, the people involved, the interactions, and how you want to feel.

As you travel your spiritual journey in this lifetime, the more you remember the real you – the spiritual you, the soul you – the more you can experience the love, joy, compassion, wisdom, kindness, beauty, patience, mercy, happiness, and generosity that the spiritual world reflects.

As you travel your physical journey and learn more about your true spiritual self, you'll experience the Five A's (which we will dive into more in later chapters):

- Attention – being heard and noticed
- Affection – giving and receiving love

- Appreciation – feeling acknowledged and valued
- Acceptance – feeling included and approved
- Allowing – safe to be yourself

The more you know your true self, the more you remember. The more you remember, the easier and better life gets, and it becomes more joyful and fulfilling. Learn to enjoy all of your life experiences, including the challenges and tough times (bumpy roads), with love in your heart. An important part to remember is that your physicalness and spiritualness are connected. As Neale Donald Walsch says, "The soul conceives, the mind creates, the body experiences. The circle is complete."

The soul conceives, the mind creates, the body experiences. The circle is complete.

~ Neale Donald Walsch

There's one Life Force and what I've learned is "What Brings You Joy Now Will Bring You Joy Over

Here." If you choose to come back to earth, there are some differences, but they're so small. What brings me joy in physical form brings me joy in non-physical form. The Circle continues.

My soul's purpose is to remember who I am, the real me, how amazing I am, to experience what I know, and that is Love. I am a spiritual being made of Love because I came from Love.

So I, being Love, try to pass it on everywhere, with everyone, all the time. One way to express this in human form is through compassionate acts of all kinds to all living things. There are many other ways to express Love. Be the example by demonstrating the 5A's through acts of kindness, forgiveness, practicing gratitude, listening, holding space, patience, to name a few. That is what real Love is; that is every soul's purpose.

You can't get it wrong. No one is keeping score or grading you. You get to choose your physical life and how you live it. Your soul is here to live in happiness, joy, and love. You can choose to live that way or not. It all depends on you and how you want to experience your physical life.

You get to choose your physical life and
how you live it. Your soul is here to live in
happiness, joy, and love. You can choose to
live that way or not.

How you learn and grow is by how you feel physically and emotionally. It's how the Universe is testing you and motivating you to study harder in this school of life and to do your best so you can move forward and be the best you can be. Make the most of your time while here. Don't leave this incomplete. Don't be one of those students who drop out of high school and have to go back and retake their least favorite class. You want the joyful feeling of fullness to keep growing in goodness and pass it on in your Circle of Life.

The Circle is a sacred symbol across many cultures and traditions, including Tibetan Buddhism. It is a universal symbol. It is said to represent eternity, unity, perfection, sacred feminine, the infinite nature of energy, and the inclusivity of the Universe.

One ritual in which the Circle's image reflects this is by drawing a circle around yourself and standing in the middle of it. The circle reveals that you are always at the center of the Universe and that sacred space continually surrounds you. Wherever you go, for the rest of your life, you're always in the middle of the Universe, and the Circle is there to divinely support you.

This quote from Helen Schucman's, *A Course in Miracles* (ACIM) defines this very well. "The circle of creation has no end. Its starting and its ending are the same. But in itself it holds the universe of all creation, without beginning and without an end." (T-28.II.1:6-8)

There is an unlimited and unending energy of Love that everyone and everything that has ever existed is a part of and connected to. The inner spiritual soul (the real you) within each human, animal, and plant is connected. We are united to all living beings. We are all one and a part of a Life Force that includes all-knowing (past, present, and future – timeless and all-dimensional). There is no beginning and no end, no better and no worse, no light and no dark, the first becomes the last and the last becomes the first because we are all equal, One, part of the Circle – and that Circle is Love, Pure Love. It is always available, surrounding us and inside of us. We are never alone.

Like a drop of water into a pool, the Circle grows and interacts with all it comes in contact. I am a drop of water, and every person, animal, plant, and thing I come in contact with throughout my life, is part of my Circle. The same is true for you.

When all human beings can grasp this conceptual idea of Circles of Life that make up the whole of Creation, we will understand the purpose of harmony. So the next time you meet someone or snuggle up to your cat or see a spider or hear a crow caw or smell lilac and you feel a sense of knowing, you are experiencing a connection to their soul.

We come to help each other and pass on love and goodness. We come to strive to make this world a better place.

Everyone has Story, a Circle, and I am about to share mine with you so that you can think of all endings as new beginnings: as parts of a Circle. I hope that my Story sheds light on your Story. I hope it enlightens, educates, inspires, enriches, and touches you in some way, so you can see that you have a Story, a Circle, and feel the oneness of the all-inclusive Universe.

CHAPTER 3

MOTHERLESS CHILD: EARLY YEARS

My Story came to a head on March 1st, 2013, at age 60, when I went to a woman's retreat in Mexico. My niece and sister-in-law had invited me to a week-long gathering titled "Sacred Sensual Splendor."

I had been in a deep depression for two years, and there were many days that I wished I could go to sleep and never wake up. My niece and sister-in-law had to coerce me to go by telling me to prepare for "an exotic adventure into your womanhood and a coming home to your Goddess essence!" But even when I arrived and started the program, I dug in my feet and was not interested in participating. That was about to change; my life was about to change. It is funny how that happens when you least expect it, but you most need life to intervene and shake you up, when you are on the verge of throwing in the towel and tapping out, or in my case, crawling in the hole I dug and pulling the dirt in around me. When you're just about to quit because you've lost the fight inside, BAM! The Universe steps in, and miracles happen.

When you're just about to quit because you've lost the fight inside, BAM! The Universe steps in, and miracles happen.

The journey began during a birthing activity at the beginning of the retreat. Taking me back to my childhood began the unraveling of what I call Pretend Mary. Simulating going through a birthing canal between huge rocks in the ocean water woke up my soul, and I started remembering who I was for a brief moment, and with that, childhood memories came flowing in.

I grew up in a small mining town in northern Minnesota where a highway ended outside my town. The weather was either freezing or humid and hot with plenty of mosquitoes. On a good day, there were 5000 people in my hometown, mostly European immigrants and either Protestant or Catholic. Everyone pretty much knew everyone else, many were related, and couples and families stayed together.

My father worked in the mine in a neighboring town, and mom stayed at home. Until I was about three years old, we lived above my grandma's house (Dad's mom). Eventually, my dad built us our home one block away. However, my early memories are at my grandma's.

On September 14th, 1953, I was born a free spirit, the Real Mary, with a lot of energy and very sensual (my sight, smell, sound, taste, touch, were amplified). I came into this world filled with pure love and joy, and seemed to notice everything from birth. My dad was well aware of my excitement for life, saying I was like a puppy, bouncing all around with my "nose" in everything. I loved to feel the wind on my face, play in the fall leaf piles, run through mud puddles, roll in the grass, and swim in the local lake.

I was the second child, born eleven months after my brother. He was born with his esophagus closed and was rushed to an emergency hospital four hours away for surgery. Back then, in the early 50s, it was a medical hardship in many ways for my parents, who were a newly married young couple, dealing with a sick child, and trying to make it financially while starting with a substantial medical bill. I came along too soon for my mother but not soon enough for my father. I say not soon enough for my father because we had a connection long before I was born.

I've been a "daddy's girl" as long as I have memories; his Baby Girl. As a child, my dad was my best friend in every way. I could talk to him about anything. I could easily play and laugh with him. I could snuggle, hug, and kiss him because I always received genuine love in return. My dad worked all day, but when he walked through the door after work, I'd be waiting there for him. He would scoop me up in his arms and swing me around while I giggled and squealed. He loved me, spent time with me, and played with me. He didn't have a lot of time because of his responsibilities – job, home, and the rest of the family. But he always made time for me. He knew I liked the Tarzan movies, so he would stay up, and at 11:45 pm, he'd wake me up to watch the movies with him. We would curl up on the couch together and cheer on Tarzan (Johnny Weissmuller) and Jane (Maureen O'Hara), and laugh at Cheetah and all the animals. We lived their adventures together; it was one of the many bonds we shared.

My father was and is the "love of my life" and "soulmate". There was never any competition, judgment, or rejection with him. I didn't have to pretend to be anyone, and I was always accepted lovingly as perfect just by being me.

I had a very different relationship with my mother. She stayed home to cook, clean, maintain our home, and attended my older brother, who, because of his medical condition, required all of her time and energy. Since we were born so close together, and she was not ready for me, there wasn't enough of her left to give me. So, I felt unloved, unwanted, and lonely. Even as a baby, I knew she did not want me. I was another one of her jobs, something that had to be taken care of.

At about two years old, maybe younger, I remember waking up every morning to the smell of our house – coffee, toast, and people. The aroma was comforting, warm, and inviting. I was a happy child, and I would jump up and down in my crib while hanging on to the slats, full of life. I'd wait for my mommy to come and get me. I was excited. I can still hear the sound of the bottom of my onesies; you know, the ones with the non-skid plastic bottoms on the feet as I paced with anticipation around my crib. There was a plastic covering over the mattress, under the sheets and blankets so that the sound of my feet on the mattress made a crinkling sound as I jumped around waiting for my mommy to come and get me, to pick me up and hold me. My brother was in the crib next to me, and he was doing the same thing. When she came in, she always went to him first. At the time, I didn't know why. So, I waited and waited for my turn. Eventually, I would lie back down, curl up, comfort myself by sucking my thumb, wait, think, and wonder.

I went through this every single day, always with the hope there would be a different outcome, but there never was. I felt it; I knew. Even a dog knows when it's loved, and I knew I wasn't. I felt abandoned.

That's when the shield of protection over my heart began to take form. I started to protect myself from getting hurt, feeling pain, and being vulnerable. Around my mom, that shield was up, and it protected me. That shield took form and strength and has stayed with me most of my life. It came down around my dad because I could express my feelings. My heart felt safe, and I was free to be the real me.

I realize now that my mom had a sick child that needed constant care and only enough energy to take care of him and keep the household running. Don't get me wrong; she always took care of my basic needs. I always looked good and was well fed and clean. My hair was always done in curls, my clothes were always clean and mended, and my mom was a good cook and an excellent baker. Our house was spotless, and so was I. I was a task to be completed like everything else in the house.

Life at home was always a series of chores needing to be done, followed by the next day of more tasks. Each day of the week had assigned activities and menus. You knew which day it was by what you were having for supper or whether laundry was being washed and ironed or the carpet vacuumed. There was no variation and certainly no time for play or being silly or spontaneous.

My mother was very controlling. Things had to be done a specific way – no deviation – and perfectly to her standards. I couldn't mess up myself, our house, or the routine, day after day. As a child, I figured out quickly that I had to obey authority figures, fit in, conform, and do everything "right" according to her; basically "be perfect." I had to obey if I wanted my needs met or not get in trouble. My natural impulses and creativity were squelched, made fun of, dismissed, or punished. Trying new things, playing, or having "fun" was not an option with my mother. I didn't feel I had the ability to make any choices, experiment and fail, try new ideas, or dance outside of the lines with love, support, positivity, and encouragement. I waited for permission as a child and carried it through into adulthood. I felt I had no power.

When I was two, Mom was busy all day long so I was alone. That is when I started living in my head. I had a little rocking chair that was a perfect size for me, so I would sit in it holding my doll, which was almost as big as I was. She was my only friend and confidante. She was a good listener. She never judged me, and she was always "there" for me. We loved each other.

I would move my little rocking chair into our hall closet, which had a window at one end and clothing rods along both sides, where all the extra, non-seasonal clothes lived. Though it smelled of cedar and mothballs, the odor was comforting to me. My dollie and I would sit for hours rocking and talking in the quiet of the closet. There was a lonely comfort there. I had a life and relationship with her. I shared my soul.

What did we talk about? All my questions were directed to her: "Why doesn't mommy like me? What's wrong with me? Why aren't I good enough to be with?" Even now, I can feel the chair's rhythmic movement. I would daydream of being a princess. I was beautiful, and I would get saved from my sadness by my Prince Charming. He would come and take me away, and we would live happily ever after. I knew there was a happily ever after. To this day, I still have mixed memories when I smell mothballs.

As a two-year-old, I was still sucking my thumb (as a pacifier) and did until I was about six years old. Then I started biting my nails. I did that until I graduated from high school. I found safety and comfort in this oral form of stimulation; it was a coping mechanism in times of stress. When I finally started growing my nails out and polishing them, I found myself picking off the polish. I used my mouth as a release of anxiety a lot, a method of coping that continued in the form of smoking.

Experts say nail-biting is a clue that you're not handling stressful, frustrating, dissatisfying, or tedious situations effectively and that you're inclined to create short-term, self-soothing habits instead of discovering positive ways to make yourself feel better in the long run. (Researchers have found that people do report that nail-biting immediately feels soothing.)

I always knew I was different than everyone else. I felt things differently, I thought about things differently, and I acted differently. I knew this because I was getting corrected or reprimanded. I said what was on my mind; I felt deeply about everything and acted it out. I loved and trusted everyone, and I was open about my feelings, thoughts, and body. In my mother's eyes, this was not okay. I remember hearing, "Watch your mouth" often. I was to be "seen and not heard." I was to act mature, and mostly I was to obey the rules. My goodness, there were so many rules, all of which felt incongruent with who I was.

Even though we never shared a close relationship, I craved my mother's love, attention, and guidance more than anything. Growing up in a motherless home leaves a big hole in your heart. There is a ceaseless drive to make oneself whole with endless yearnings. It is even emptier when the mother is physically there but emotionally unavailable. I needed my mother. But I felt rejected and unwanted. Many aspects of my "normal" healthy development were missing, and what was available was distorted, leaving me with no self-love, misbeliefs, and poor self-esteem. Being a motherless child, I felt a loss of love and approval and plenty of rejection. As an adult, I learned to compensate for this. I was always and desperately seeking the 5 A's: attention, affection, appreciation, acceptance, and allowing from others (mostly men).

I can now, after 60 years, finally accept this, understanding that she did the best she could, and I forgive her. Coming to this realization has not been easy. As a young child, I was a sponge, open and pure, with only feelings and no understandings. Painful yet resilient, even as I write this, I can feel it, but I no longer own the pain. That is the past, and I've accepted it and released it.

I was never hurtful or mean. I cared about everyone and everything. My heart was filled with love and joy, but as I got older, I had to stifle myself and be like everyone expected me to be, so I started to become the Pretend Mary. This worked well on the outside, but I was starting to become sad and numb inside. What a hurdle of misbeliefs I had to overcome once I decided to be the real me. It's a process that I am still working on.

We moved into our new house when I was four years old. That year, I started kindergarten. I begged my mom to let me go to school when my brother started. I knew I didn't want to be alone at home with my mom, and I think she let me go because she was glad to "get rid of me" and didn't have to be alone with me either.

School was fun for me. I am a very social person and loved being around other kids. My need for attention required that I be the center of it. Modeling my mother's behaviors, I was controlling and demanding. That got me in some trouble with the teacher, and one time, I was put in time out.

I came to school one day wearing a beautiful, new purple floral dress I'd worn for Easter. I thought I was a princess, and I'm sure I let everyone know, not realizing how anyone else felt. We were painting that day. As I was happily painting at my easel, being extra careful not to get any of the paint on me, one of the boys came up to me with paint on his hands and rubbed them down the front of my dress, ruining it. He wanted to hurt me, and he did. I burst out crying and had to go home. I was scared of what my mother would say and do. My dress was ruined, and I knew she would be angry. She yelled at me for being careless. At the time, I felt like it was my fault. Believing I was at fault was a choice I made. I now know it was just childhood behaviors, things kids do to each other. No one was at fault. This was a life lesson for me, a lesson in forgiveness – for myself, the boy, and my mom.

Our family grew. Along came a baby sister, then another sister, and finally a younger brother. I was seven years old when he was born. We were seven good but very different people; a strange group of individuals making up my family. We loved each other because that was what families do but did not model deeply loving relationships.

We were expected to behave acceptably, which we did despite the usual sibling bickering over something silly and insignificant that at the time seemed monumental. We were put together for occasions, like our daily supper meal, where we each had our spot at the kitchen table. However, as soon as we finished the meal, I would get on the telephone and call one of my friends. Our telephone in the living room had a long cord attached to the phone that could reach into the closet. I would call a friend, take the phone into the closet, and girl talk. Talking could easily go on for hours until my mother would yell, "Get off that damn phone."

I have no recollection of family discussions or conversations about anything meaningful, insightful, or interactive. We never talked about our feelings. We just existed in this same space together and interacted as necessary to get through each day. We were a family, but we weren't friends. The conversations I remember were about what went on during the day, who did what, who was going to do what, small talk. Pretend Mary was taking hold.

My mom liked to correct me and yell. Why was she like this toward me and not my other siblings? Why wasn't I good enough? Thank goodness for my dad. He saw it, and he felt it, too. He did his best to show me love, give me his time and attention, listen to me, play with me, and laugh with me. He always made me feel wanted, deserving of love and happiness. He enjoyed playing and liked to tease me and tickle me.

We spent hours together in his workshop. He went there to get away from her, usually after an argument. I was always the one who went with him. He would be doing some woodworking, and I would sit alongside his bench, and we would talk about everything and anything, both of us trying to put her out of our minds. I think she was jealous of the relationship shared by my dad and me. She didn't understand that he and I were alike, and we needed the same thing – her. She tried to poison me against him but instead, succeeded in poisoning me against myself.

One of the few interactions I remember having with my mother when I was eight years old was her trying to teach me to make my family's traditional dessert, Slovanian poticia, a type of strudel. I was so excited to learn, and my mom was finally going to teach me. I even got to put on an apron.

She had already prepared the dough, so I was going to help her stretch it across the kitchen table. Our table sat 8-10 people; it was huge. The kitchen chairs had to be moved so we could efficiently work around the table. My mom laid an old sheet on top of the table, draping it down the sides. I got to spread the flour, smoothing it ever so carefully and evenly over the top of the sheet. My hands were in it. I was making poticais!

My mom placed the big ball of dough in the middle and with a floured rolling pin, starting rolling it flat, moving it in all directions from the center of the table. I sprinkled flour on the dough ball as it grew. Inside I was having so much fun; on the outside, I was serious and concentrating on doing everything right that she asked of me.

Once the dough was rolled out as flat as my mom could get it, we gently used our fingers to stretch it over the table and down the sides (kind of like a pizza maker stretching his dough). I wasn't experienced and had little fingers, so I kept tearing the dough as I pulled it.

"No holes in the dough!" My mother yelled. I tried to pinch the pieces together and smooth it out to fix it and make it better, but my mother was frustrated and angry. She yelled, "Just stop. You're not doing it right. I don't want your help. Go away.

I'll do it myself." My heart sank. My excitement turned from joy to heartbreak in an instant.

I took off my apron and slipped out of the kitchen as my mom continued as if nothing happened. But something happened to me. That was the last time until well into adulthood that I ever put on an apron and attempted to bake anything. I didn't make my first batch of Christmas cookies until I was 64 years old.

Throughout my childhood, I was afraid to try things. At school, I stayed in the background for fear of not being good enough, not even getting out there and trying, in fear of having others do what my mom did. I couldn't handle the possibility that the "not good enough" message would be reinforced by others and I would again feel rejected.

I was raised in a very Catholic household, so every Sunday, we dressed in our best clothes and went to church as a family. The day before church, I went to confession so I could receive communion on Sunday. I had to be absolved of all my sins. I also attended catechism weekly. All students were released from school to walk to their church for religious instruction. The nuns taught us, and they were very strict. I don't remember what I said or did, but one time I got smacked hard on the knuckles with a ruler. This is where I learned that the all-loving God I believed in could be vengeful, and based on how he felt about you and your behavior or what sins you committed, you were either going to Heaven or Hell after you died.

As a kid who believed she wasn't good enough, I was sure I was going to Hell. Needless to say, I tried to be perfect, to be good, and do things "right" because I wanted to go to Heaven. However, since I couldn't be perfect, I was going to Hell. I couldn't reconcile in my mind that a loving God could be punishing. I couldn't make sense of it.

Later, as a young adult, I left the church teachings. I couldn't imagine a God that was so strict and unloving. So, I started looking into other religious beliefs. I always believed in a God, but I wanted to believe in a good, all-loving God.

I got away from any formal religion and wasn't a "religious" person, but I always tried to do my best and be a good person. I went through my entire adulthood this way. I prayed at times, I was thankful and giving, I was kind, and I was forgiving and not judgmental of others, to the best of my ability. I learned this over time, through experiences, self-growth, and basically something I felt inside, something I just knew. My soul knew.

Then there's also the whole concept of loyalty. As a child, I was the loyal daughter, though this changed as I moved into my teenage years.

Did you ever watch the movie *The Wizard of Oz*? Do you remember the foot soldiers for the witch? They were loyal, they fought for her, they protected her, and they obeyed her rules. They behaved mechanically. They aligned with her reality. She said, this is who is bad, and this is who is good, or this is what is bad, and this is what is good. They said, "Yes, yes, yes!" They followed her every wish and command until she was exorcised and they flew and soared freely; they left, scattered. They sang, they danced, they were free.

The Loyalty Factor is a form of brainwashing. I was a loyal child, a sponge, yearning for any love and attention. I absorbed it all just like a dutiful foot soldier. I said yes on the outside but on the inside, I was screaming no.

The Loyalty Factor is a form of brainwashing. I was a loyal child, a sponge, yearning for any love and attention. I absorbed it all just like a dutiful foot soldier. I said yes on the outside but on the inside, I was screaming no.

Motherless love has been and still is the core of all my issues, misbeliefs, and fears around aging, my body, my need for control, need for approval, and pretending to be someone people would like – being accepted and not rejected, not being good enough, feeling unlovable, guilt, shame, and self-doubt. I learned as a child that to be loved and accepted, I had to do certain things correctly. I learned that love and acceptance were conditional. I thought that if I could do something perfectly, I would earn the love I craved. All of those things made up Pretend Mary, and I tried hard throughout my life to be that person, not realizing I was chasing an impossible task and that love came from the inside out and not the other way around. Instead of creating from the inside, I was reacting to the outside.

Instead of creating from the inside, I was

reacting to the outside.

CHAPTER 4

POISON: MIDDLE YEARS

I went to a small grade school that was connected to the junior high and high school. In my early years, a community college was also connected, so it was common to see all age groups at school. I was in a class of 139 students, and we went through school together until graduation, give or take a few students.

I tried to be a teacher pleaser, teacher's pet, believing that I would be loved for being myself if I did everything asked. I soon realized that I couldn't replace the need for my mother's love and approval with my teacher's.

School also had too many rules. Things had to be done the teacher's way. "Do what I tell you to do. You need to settle down. Stop talking." The expectations were endless. I was supposed to act a certain way, do what was asked, and conform. Just like at home with my mother, school was more of the same thing. What I was learning was that society and the culture I lived in wanted me to conform, but I didn't understand the expectations they wanted me to meet.

I began forgetting that I was a soul. Becoming Pretend Mary and being someone that others wanted me to be, made much of my school years a blur.

"Why is everybody telling me what to do? Why can't I do it my way?" were questions I would ask myself alone at night. I would try to figure out why I was different, why I saw things differently and thought differently, but I couldn't and eventually would cry myself to sleep. The next day, I'd try again try to be the person everyone wanted me to be. Of course, the next day and the day after that and the day after that were all the same.

My mom always judged us kids and had high expectations. She knew how to manipulate us and tried to instill competitiveness in us, pitting us against each other. She always saw us as separate and treated us each differently. Mom compared me to my siblings and the neighborhood kids. "Why can't you be more like your brother? Or Susie? Jean helps her mother; why can't you? Look how nice your sister behaves. You need to do better in school, like Bonnie." The comparisons, judgments, and fault-finding comments were a daily event.

My mother judged herself worst of all, and I internalized her insecurities as my own. She judged others by their cooking, housekeeping skills, behaviors, and their families. I judged other people by their appearance, weight, hairstyle, clothes, how they spoke, and how they acted. I made negative assumptions about those I judged. They were lazy, they didn't care about themselves, or they didn't have a mirror. I said many times as a young teen that I would not have an overweight friend. My rationale was that they couldn't do the physical things that I enjoyed doing. These were all the very things I was insecure about within myself. I judged myself, worst of all.

We are human. We all judge occasionally. Why? It may feel good at the time, but it never lasts. When I looked within myself as I judged, I saw that I was really looking at what I was feeling about myself.

> When I looked within myself as I judged, I saw
> that I was really looking at what I was feeling
> about myself.

Now, I try to remember the difference between judgment and observation. I strive to remain neutral in situations instead of forming opinions.

Teenage years are rough with hormonal changes, low self-esteem, judgmental peer pressure, and many influences from the outside world. I grew into an angry teenager with a quick temper that was often directed toward my dad because I took my frustrations out on the one person I loved the most and was closest to. I felt safe with him; safe enough to vent. I knew he would love me through my outbursts.

But my father's acceptance had never been enough. I craved my mother's love and attention but only got it when I acted out, got angry, or did something wrong – the very things that made me feel "less than" and what I was missing in me. I was needy, wanting my mother's love, acting out to get noticed, angry, blaming, hurting, and repeating. My pattern of behavior was a vicious cycle, one I felt I had no control over.

Although my anger found many targets, it was always meant for my mother. I blamed my mother as the source of my pain and frustration. I did not feel safe with her. I was afraid of her. I hated her. I thought there was something wrong with me because I could never meet my mother's expectations and earn her love. Eventually, the blame shifted to myself. I continued blaming myself as an adult.

I regret taking my anger out on my father. I didn't want to hurt him; I wanted to hurt her and hurt myself. I know now that my dad understands this and has forgiven me. Although he said, "There's nothing to forgive," I am trying to forgive myself. Forgiveness is a gift you give to yourself, and I had to learn to choose this for me.

Forgiveness is a gift you give to yourself, and I had to learn to choose this for me.

Ever since I can remember being around adults, I was compared, rated, graded, and judged on practically everything I did or didn't do, and then I was urged to do the same thing to other people. I always felt like I needed to compete with my siblings, then my friends, and later in life with my husband, coworkers, neighbors, everyone. I was always trying to be better or smarter than everyone. I wanted to be the best at everything, or I had to be right.

Teachers, parents, family members, television, and society drilled this into me, and I did my best to be that person. I took on these beliefs because I was expected to, and it was easier to follow along and be like everyone else. But inside, I wasn't like everyone else. I am me, I am unique, and these two sets of beliefs were at odds with each other. How could I fit in and still be the real me? I wasn't strong enough inside to do it, so I conformed to those expectations, those misbeliefs. The result was the Pretend Mary.

I got yelled at a lot for talking in class. Talking got me the attention I needed. After each incident (and there were many), I would shut my mouth and sit quietly, trying to be focused. This is hard for me because I am stimulated by almost everything. I've been referred to as a butterfly, flitting from thought to thought, thing to thing, never lighting for any length of time.

The Pretend Mary tried but was not happy and was often angry and rebellious throughout school, but I continued to follow these beliefs and tried to fit in while I was around other people. I was confused and questioned everything. The more confused I was, the more frustrated I got, and the more rejected I felt for just being me. This manifested into a need to control and be right. Control took the form of obsessive-compulsiveness in organizing my things – my clothes, my room, my space, my body, my hair, my makeup, my physicality. (This grew into a severe problem that I will discuss later.)

I became two people – one smiling, trying to be a perfectionist and people pleaser, playing the game as Pretend Mary on the outside and hurting on the inside. The other was a confused, sad, and lonely little girl. The result was being overwhelmed, moody, argumentative, and angry. I took it out on my parents and siblings but mostly beat up on myself. Just like I did as a child, I spent a lot of time alone in my room. I still didn't understand what was wrong with me, why I was different.

One day at school, a teacher told me I was too much of a free spirit. What did that mean? I had been sent to get some paper from another teacher's classroom. I started down the hall to her room but ended up walking all around the school, inside and outside. It felt good to get out and see what was going on. I liked peeking in the other classrooms. I knew I would eventually get the paper, but I wanted to wander around first, doing it my way. My way was more entertaining, more fun.

By the time high school rolled around, I had perfected the Pretend Mary, making life seem much easier. My self-esteem wasn't healthy enough to be real. I was afraid to be vulnerable. So the rebellious teenager continued acting out when I couldn't get attention by being good – dressing in short skirts, putting on forbidden makeup when I got to school, sneaking booze from my parents, smoking cigarettes (which I didn't like), smoking pot (which was cool). I tried to fit in with the cool kids but was never quite able to do so. I was tall, skinny, a bit awkward, and pimply-faced. I never felt attractive in any way. I felt ugly and unwanted a lot of the time. But I needed people, I needed friends, I needed to be accepted. So, I kept trying. I never had a boyfriend in high school but had "crushes" on at least a dozen boys. I was not asked to any dances but attended them all. I was not asked to prom and wondered what was wrong with me, never realizing, "who would want a relationship with a fake person?"

I became Pretend Mary for most of my life.

CHAPTER 5

STRUGGLE: ADULTHOOD

I first met my husband the day before my 17th birthday. He was almost 24 years old and had recently returned from Vietnam with PTSD and drinking. From that point on, we have primarily been together. We were both second-born children to mothers who were controlling, critical, judgmental, and not happy. No wonder we both needed to control. My need for control expressed itself in my body and immediate environment. His expressed itself in the people and situations surrounding him.

I enjoyed the attention from this older, experienced man. He is a very popular, handsome, intelligent man. I was none of those, or so I believed. I was a small-town girl who was not worldly. I was naive. I never had a boyfriend, yet I was always interested in boys and was a big flirt. I had no experience with love, other than the love I had for my father; it was the only love I knew – safe, consistent, and unconditional. So, I did not know how to love anyone else or to be loved by anyone else.

We started dating, fell in love (what I perceived love to be), got married, and have been together for 48 years. We have built successful careers, a beautiful home, and had a mostly happy life. We were busy and occupied and spent all of our free time together. He is a hard worker, very generous, and was dedicated to making a comfortable life for us. He is also a strong man, a natural and skilled leader.

I was the perfect follower: devoted. I looked up to him and trusted that everything he did and said was right and the best for us. But because of my deep-seated belief that I wasn't good enough or loveable, I internalized every negative comment and judgmental observation. I absorbed comments about others as if there were directed to me, believing they were about me.

I was striving to be perfect. Whatever he wanted, whatever he needed in all aspects, I tried to accommodate. Never once did I question him or his beliefs because I knew he loved me and took good care of me.

I would have done anything to keep him because he was my first boyfriend, and I believed I would never get another if I lost him. I became whatever he wanted me to be. I tried to be the perfect girlfriend and then the ideal wife. I had no clue who I was or what I wanted for my life. I was grateful someone even wanted me because I was nobody special (or so I believed at that time). My self-esteem was low and insecurities high. When I dated and married him, I always said to myself, "I wonder what he sees in me. I wonder why he picked me? I wonder why he loves me?" I could never understand.

I put him in the role of an authority figure, which meant I felt I needed to do things the way he did to be loved and accepted. Pleasing my husband was all-important to receive the 5 A's. But in doing so, I willingly gave him my power.

So, that is how I let my past misbeliefs and low self-esteem run my life. I was still the Pretend Mary, trying to please and go along with all my perceived expectations. I felt I needed to fit a perfect image of beauty and behavior to be the ideal woman that society defined. These expectations are impossible for any one woman to attain. I realize now it took a lot of thought, time, and effort to live up to the expectations I took on. I just ran on autopilot and did it. I didn't know any different. I accepted it all as normal.

I remember when we first got married, my husband said, "Gaining weight is grounds for divorce." I am tall, 5'8", and have a fast metabolism. I have never been fat. But if I gained any weight, he made a comment. If I lost too much weight, he commented. So, I tried always to look perfect (or what I perceived perfect to be based on television and magazine idols). I always wore makeup, coordinated my clothes, styled my hair, had the perfect tan, straightened my teeth – the perfect look, the perfect wife. I believed that's what would make me loveable – the perfect Pretend Mary. However, I was mentally still a teenager being raised and molded.

My husband liked to comment on people's physical appearance. These judgmental comments were constant. Although they were not directed toward me, the messages I internalized were, "Don't let this happen to you. If you do, people will say those things about you. You won't be good enough. You won't be loveable." It was always in my mind, "What do people think about me? What are they seeing? Do I look perfect?"

Thinking back, even as a child and teenager, I internalized the concept of physical perfection; it was the one thing I could control. If I could get close to perfection, then maybe people would like me. So, having a baby was out of the question. I couldn't possibly allow my body to change. "I could get stretch marks. My nipples would turn brown." I wouldn't be perfect anymore. Although no one ever said this to me, it was always in my mind.

I internalized the concept of physical
perfection; it was the one thing I could
control. If I could get close to perfection,
then maybe people would like me.

For over 45 years, I carried this expectation, never realizing that I was doing it or asking myself why I was doing it or how it affected me. I was simply too busy to take a close look at the real me. I didn't even know there was a Real Mary. I didn't realize until I was 59 years old that I spent my whole life pretending to be the person that other people wanted me to be in order to be accepted and not rejected.

The need to be perfect manifested itself in other ways through the need to be right and control the things in my life that I could. As a high school counselor, my office was neat, my files were meticulous, and I ran my department with my hand in everything. Detail and accuracy were essential, and that fit right into my controlling way. As controlling as I was at work, I was more so at home.

I found control in the form of obsessions: a compulsion for neatness, spotlessness, and cleanliness. Everything had a place, and everything was in its place. As a little girl, all my stuffed animals had their proper places on my dresser. They had to remain in the exact place and never be moved for me to feel comfortable and safe. All my clothes in my closet had to be in order, on the proper hanger, and always used and returned to the same place.

I still do this. Nothing is allowed to be threadbare, no flaws or hairs, shoes are always polished after every use. My drawers of clothes are also arranged in perfect order, and everything is in its proper place – socks, panties, bras all color-coordinated. Outfits are always color coordinated and perfectly matched – top to bottom. My toiletries are all organized according to use. Every closet, every cabinet, every drawer in every room in my house is organized, and every item has its place and must always go back to that exact place after use. No variation. I have control over all of my things.

For years, I found comfort and safety by being organized and having a strict routine. Nothing was ever out of place on me or in my environment. Our home was perfect. Every item in it was organized, in its place, and hygienically clean (almost to the point of being unused). The windows were washed inside and out. The exterior was washed yearly – house, patios, decks; it never ended. Our yard did not have a weed; it was raked, and every shrub, plant, and tree manicured.

Company did not come over very often, but when they did, I would cringe knowing they were using things in my house and things were no longer perfect. I was uncomfortable, and I'm sure they were as well. Most entertaining was done in the warmer weather when we could be outdoors. My husband likes things neat, too, and for the most part, he put up with my obsessions and let me have my way, a path of least resistance.

There was a lot of frustration in me, and I cried a lot in my adulthood. I was putting so much pressure on myself that pretending was getting more and more challenging to maintain. All this comparing and worrying about what others thought was only hurting me. I wasn't happy. I gave my power away instead of taking responsibility for all I said, did, and thought. I ended up blaming others or the situation.

All this comparing and worrying about what others thought was only hurting me. I wasn't happy. I gave my power away instead of taking responsibility for all I said, did, and thought.

Some of these behaviors continue to this day. However, I have relaxed on the housecleaning, personal grooming, and now everything gets used. I work on these obsessions and am slowly releasing and letting go. I have realized that things are not important, people are, and so is living life with ease and peace.

Today, I work every day to remember the Real Mary. Even though I am 65 years old, I am happy to be going through this part of my Story, My Circle. I am grateful I did not skip this stage. I had to experience exactly what I experienced to find the real me. I know this is my life's journey, for the gifts/lessons I need to receive. They have helped me in so many ways. I would not be the person I am today without having gone through all that I did. I was exactly where I was supposed to be, doing exactly what I did to be the best person I can be. I am so very grateful to my husband for all these experiences. Thank you!!!

I created Pretend Mary to meet my needs for the 5As because I didn't think I could get them by being the real me. I could only get them by being someone I believed others accepted. For years, I thought Pretend Mary was the Real Mary. I never stopped my busy life to take a close look at myself. I was immersed in being human and living a life I thought was "normal". I looked around at others, friends, family, television, and I knew I was similar. Yes, I had my quirks but didn't everybody? Some people have to get all A's in school, and some people need to earn a lot of money, while some people need fame. I needed to be perfect, and I accepted that as part of being me.

Throughout it all, I never asked myself if I was happy. I believed I was. I was living the American dream – I had a good job that I liked, a happy marriage to a handsome, charismatic man, lots of friends, a full social life, a model's body, a beautiful home, no serious money worries; I was moving forward and being productive. I had it all. Friends would say that they envied my life because they, too, thought I had it all. I agreed with them because I felt the same way. My life was blessed.

I never questioned my life or asked any of the important self-reflective questions: Who am I? Why am I here? What is my purpose? I didn't understand my need for attention, acceptance, appreciation, affection, and allowing. I wasn't interested in changing my life or myself. Source, God, Universe, Divine Life, Creator knew I wasn't ready. I needed a "wake up" call, and I had no clue it was coming. And what a wake-up call to get: depression.

CHAPTER 6

DEPRESSION

I didn't understand what true depression was until I retired from my job at age 52. I have a Master's degree in Counseling Education from the University of Puget Sound and for 22 years, I worked as a high school counselor. I helped, guided, encouraged, and inspired students every day. I loved my students, co-workers, and my job. I was good at it. I had an active life and social circle. I attended numerous functions, workshops, and activities with my co-workers and friends. I looked forward to work every day and was happy. I felt Appreciation and Acceptance, as well as the other A's in my career.

I was fulfilled but ready to start the next phase of my life. So, when my husband retired, I retired. However, I wasn't prepared. Not having something to do every day, I thought I would play and party for the rest of my life. I envisioned traveling in our RV with my husband, living the good life, without a care in the world. But that's not what happened to me. I went from people needing and wanting my time and attention to nothing. What a shock!

Now, I had plenty of time (all day, every day) to fill and no audience, students, co-workers, or friends. My work met the 5A's for me, so when I retired, I had to find another way to meet those needs. Once again, I was meeting them from the outside in and not the inside out.

I no longer felt needed or had a purpose except to play. I didn't have to worry about money, so we moved our RV to a beach town and parked it. It became my getaway. I met new people there and started to party, real hard, without any regard to consequences. I only wanted to have fun. I was self-abusive, and I thought I was happy, but I was escaping into a crazy world. This went on for five years. It was fun, and I had plenty of people who were willing to play with me. I had many happy times with wonderful people that are still a part of my life. I've always managed to keep a balance. Even though I partied hard, I always kept some form of control. Even so, this behavior was an inner attack, a cry for help, an internal call to myself. My self-esteem was at an all-time low, and I knew I couldn't continue this behavior.

... this behavior was an inner attack, a cry for help, an internal call to myself. My self-esteem was at an all-time low, and I knew I couldn't continue this behavior.

As I had in the past, I needed to control something, so I thought I would change the one thing that I could: my body. That was the only area I felt I had any power over. I thought this was what I needed to be happy.

At 54 years old, the aging process began in earnest. It started with a little sag in my butt. I was visiting a girlfriend in Florida, and I was changing into my bikini. She came up behind me, flicked my butt, and said, "You're getting a little loose back here. I think you need to exercise to tighten it up." It just so happened at the time, I was walking five miles a day and was in great shape.

At that moment, I realized I couldn't exercise the aging process away. I had excess skin on my slim frame when I never fluctuated more than 10 pounds; that didn't make sense to me. Immediately my mind took me to "two bulldogs in a bag." But the reality was there. The gravity that comes with age was happening. My goodness, I had to do something about that.

During the same time, I noticed I could feel the bottoms of my breasts touching my chest. Oh no, "Cooper's droop" was starting. Excess skin seemed to be appearing in many places, and I became obsessed with it. So, I met with a plastic surgeon and had a "Mommy makeover" – butt lift, breast augmentation, tummy tuck, and a lower facelift. I had to fix what I could so I would look perfect once again, so people would like me, accept me, and not talk badly about me. I thought I could build my self-esteem from the outside.

I felt wonderful afterward. I was physically rebuilt and looking great. But the feeling didn't last. Just like partying or shoe shopping, it was a temporary high, happiness from the outside. I realized it didn't fill the void inside me or give my life the meaning I wanted. The emptiness was still there.

After retiring, five years of partying, and one year of surgeries and recovery, I still didn't know what I wanted to do, and I sure didn't know how to make myself happy. I kept seeking. I thought a new career, one that involved interacting with people, was the answer. I needed a way to meet my 5A's.

I enrolled in ABC Bartender School, a two-week bartending class. I was excited about this new adventure. In the first few days, I found it challenging. It was fast-paced, and there was so much memorization. I thought I would quit. But I wasn't going to be a Bartender School dropout. I decided I would commit to it and do my very best.

I had to memorize 100+ cocktails, shots, and martinis, their ingredients, how to make each drink, the glass, and garnish. I was timed to make ten different drinks in five minutes and complete a 100-question written test. I performed at the top of my class. I was elated. I had set my mind on my goal, and I achieved it. The day I got my certificate, I went to a temp agency and got hired. I was a hired bartender! My first job was a week later. It was a wedding, and I was the bar back (back up to the head bartender). I had to buy a long-sleeved black shirt, black slacks, and a black apron. My instructions and location were emailed to me. I was ready and excited. I arrived an hour early.

It was a 97-degree day, and the venue was downtown in a hall with no air conditioning. Because I was early, I was asked to help move furniture, set up tables, and unload beer, wine, and equipment cases. Not what I thought I would be doing, but I was happy to comply and do my best while trying not to get too sweaty. When the bartender came, we set up our bar. It looked beautiful, and we were ready. As the guests arrived, I chatted, served, and smiled at everyone. My first customer gave me a $5 tip. The bartender informed me that it was a no-host bar and we could not accept tips, which he took from me. No problem, I was happy doing my job despite the heat.

When dinner was served and the bar slowed, I was asked to wait tables and, following dinner, to clear the tables. I couldn't carry a heavy tray, but I graciously did as I was told to the best of my ability.

When the guests left, I took down tables, put the furniture back where it was, sorted and stacked dishes, and helped load the truck. Finally, I was asked to sort out the recycling. This meant going through all the garbage, digging out all the bottles and cans among the leftover food and cake, a nasty job, to say the least. Certainly not what I expected, but again, I did what I was asked. After nine hours of hot and hard work, I was getting ready to leave when the catering company owner, impressed with my work, complimented me and said he wanted me for future jobs. I knew I didn't want to work for his company again, so I thanked him and told him I thought this work was better suited to a younger person. When I received my paycheck, I earned $59.

I was so discouraged, and a few days later, I returned the clothes. I was done. I'd had high hopes of a fun way to get some attention and appreciation and earn some money. But instead, I felt used.

Three weeks later, the temp agency called and asked if I would be interested in a bartending job at a lovely theater downtown, one I went to frequently. After a bit of soul searching and not wanting to be a quitter, I decided I would "get back on the horse" and try again. I thought this new job would be a better experience with interesting people and an upscale venue. I bought a black shirt, black slacks and this time I needed a black tie. I was excited and set. The day before I was to work, I had not received my email with instructions, so I called the agency. "Oh, I'm sorry. Didn't I tell you that job got canceled!" said the receptionist. I was stunned, devastated.

A couple of days later, I returned the black shirt, black slacks, and the black tie. I don't know why this hit me so hard, but it did. It felt like the last straw. I went from excited to emotionally numb. I just crumbled, feeling worthless, unwanted, and unworthy. I was drained. For the first time in my life, I wanted out of life.

I went into a depression. I felt as though I had failed. Over the next year, I went from a bubbly, happy, and social lady to a shell who spent most of her day in bed. I thought it was menopause hormonal imbalance and that I would get through it. But it got progressively worse. I withdrew from life. By the time I was 57, I didn't recognize myself. I was a recluse. I felt I had no sense of purpose. I remember waking up morning after morning and saying, "Damn, I woke up!"

This feeling was so overwhelming and foreign to me that I didn't know what to do. It felt like it happened suddenly, but looking back, I realize that it crept up on me, little by little, until I was engulfed and partially bedridden. I had stopped enjoying life. For the first time, I was quite content to be alone. But it wasn't healthy for me because I was always a very social person, a people person.

My husband and friends tried to reach out and suggested I see a counselor. But I was a counselor! For years, I'd helped others sort out their problems. I thought I should be able to figure it out for myself. But I couldn't.

My one saving grace was that I walked almost every day. Miles and hours and listening to music, which was the only practice I enjoyed and, in hindsight, saved me. So, I would wake up every day crying because I woke up. After beating myself up and feeling sorry for myself and my life, I would go for a walk. It gave me hope. I never lost faith in myself; it was my strength. I kept telling myself that there is a reason I had to go through this, and I would know what it was when it was over. Was it because I needed to experience sadness after living such a blessed life? Was I having some sort of Karmic experience? Why did I have to be so depressed? What could I possibly learn from this pain? What was going on with me?

I never lost faith in myself; it was my strength. I kept telling myself that there is a reason I had to go through this, and I would know what it was when it was over.

Thinking about what was happening made the pain worse. I was 58 and trying to figure out who I was and where I was going with my life. What was my next purpose? Why was I still alive? There must be a reason. I didn't feel I could talk to anybody about what I was going through. I didn't understand it, so how could anyone else? It was easier and more comfortable to isolate myself. It was safe.

And so, the search began. I started getting all the medical tests to see if what was happening to me was physiological or psychological. Time and time again, all the medical tests, blood work, etc., told me I was healthy. So it was psychological. Was it because of me, because of my relationships, because of my life? What was making me feel so depressed? I finally had a little counseling, but nothing seemed to surface to make me change or feel any different.

The reasons why I went into what I now know was depression became very clear as time went by. Spending so much time alone, I slowed down, and started to think. I looked deep into myself and asked questions such as, "Who is the Real Mary? Why are you here? What is your purpose? Why are you so sad and empty? What would make you happy?"

In spending time with myself, I realized I felt a significant loss at that period in my life. I was in a transition. A transition is often precipitated by trauma, grief, or loss. What was I losing? I had everything anyone could want – a beautiful home, a loving husband, a new body, a comfortable lifestyle in every way, and the freedom to do whatever I wanted to do whenever I wanted to do it. What was missing? Why was I feeling such a profound loss that it put me into a depression that kept me in the dark mental place and an isolated social/physical place?

What was I losing?

Then it came to me. Until that point, I hadn't realized how I measured my importance through my career. I no longer had teenage student minds to mold, nurture, encourage, and inspire. So now what?

Without my job to occupy my days, I began to use my time to look into myself, studying me. The more I delved, the more I wanted to find myself. I knew I was the only one who could change what I was allowing to happen to me. So, I decided to do just that.

I was tired of being tired and sad. I remember lying in bed, crying and praying. I felt helpless, so I asked God for help. Finally, I started to take some control. I changed to a healthy diet, added vitamins and minerals to that, and continued walking. I felt healthy physically but not mentally. I began reading self-help books and listening to uplifting audiobooks while walking. I was desperate to make a change, but I didn't know how.

When I was in my depression, I had no aim and no purpose, and for that period of time, I had no will to go on. I wanted my life to end. But I now know it wasn't supposed to end at that time; I had more to do in this life. One of the things I had to do was to feel the deadness inside through the depression, and not only live through it but also to rise above it and strengthen my spirituality. I found the lesson, the gift, in going through this depression. Life wanted more for me; Source, God, Universe, Divine Life, Creator wanted more for me; and I wanted more for me.

I found the lesson, the gift, in going through this depression. Life wanted more for me; Source, God, Universe, Divine Life, Creator wanted more for me; and I wanted more for me.

Going through all of this, there always was a glimmer of Hope. I knew I wouldn't be in this stuck place forever. I knew, deep inside, that this depression (because I could finally call it what it was) wouldn't last forever, and eventually, I would be "me" again. Little did I know, I would never be "me" again, and that was a good thing.

In hindsight, my depression was my blessing. It was a catalyst for me to slow down and observe myself, and I mean all aspects of myself. I had never taken any time to look at myself or ask myself any questions about who I am, why I do the things I do, behave the way I do, believe the things I do, feel the way I feel. Until that point, I had never examined the real me at all to see if any of the things I mentioned were true, if they made me happy, if they added to my joy and self-love, if they made me a better person. I needed the contrast of the depression to find my greater joy. I didn't appreciate it for what it was at the time, but I sure appreciate it now. Without that sadness, I would not have found my happiness.

Finally, I felt I could do something. I could take control of myself and face my loss over Pretend

Mary's death because I was opening myself up for the emergence of the Real Mary. And let me tell you, Pretend Mary didn't go down without a fight. It was fierce and gut-wrenching.

I was starting to experience a transformation, and I wasn't even aware of it as it was happening. If you know anything about the process of the chrysalis, it is a total transformation called metamorphosis. The caterpillar spins a cocoon. While it's in there, it digests itself by dissolving all of its tissues in preparation to rebuild itself into a butterfly about four weeks later.

I was the caterpillar, and a butterfly was about to emerge. The Pretend Mary was about to transform into the Real Mary.

The day before the women's retreat in Mexico that would change everything, I went to get a haircut. I wasn't looking forward to the trip; it wasn't a vacation or a getaway. My niece was a facilitator at the retreat, and she'd asked me to attend.

I was sitting in my hairdresser's chair, struggling with going on the trip, looking at my reflection in the mirror in front of me. The mirror was huge at 6x4 feet, with a thick wooden frame. I could see my entire body in it. I was looking at a huge sad Mary, someone I didn't even recognize. I made a quick observation of her body; the way she sat, how her feet rested on the chair's rung, how her hands lay limply in her lap. It was her face that I was drawn to, that I lingered on. I observed objectively, like looking at someone I'd never seen before. And I hadn't ever seen this version of me. I was looking at a stranger.

I received this with my mind but what was different was that I was observing and witnessing it with my soul, the Real Mary. I was having an awakening. I stared until my hairdresser came back to my chair, and then I said, "I feel like my pilot light has gone out and I don't know how to re-light it. I can't even find the damn matches," as I continued to stare at that reflection.

But after that moment of clarity, I went into the Pretend Mary mode of being and didn't look at why I was feeling this way or how I got there. I just continued to blab about nothing, pretending to be okay. It's easy for me to go there; it's my default position: "don't make anyone uncomfortable; make sure people like you." I wasn't ready to take a close look at myself and do the work. I wasn't prepared or equipped at this point in my life. I knew I would one day; I knew I would find my way. I knew I would get tired of pretending and let go of what other people thought and realize what is important is what I think. I knew the work had to come from the inside out. I knew I could do this. I would do this. I had faith; God loved me. I would learn to love myself.

Coming out of depression and remembering me, my soul, the Real Mary, started with glimpses, like the one at the hairdressers. A little step ahead, then several steps back. The journey was beginning. Each time I went backward, it was hard to start moving again. But I did. I forced myself, a little at a time, which took months and months. The whole time I was doing this, I gained skills, picking up tools along the way. I was slowly working at turning myself back on.

CHAPTER 7
MEXICO

When my niece and sister-in-law invited me to the Vividly Woman retreat in Trocones, Mexico, they said, "It will be fun. We can play." I was just going through the motions of living and didn't feel like doing much of anything. But coming from a counseling background, I thought it would be interesting, and I'd never experienced this type of retreat, so I agreed to go, mostly because I loved them.

I hadn't thought much about the trip until it was almost time to leave. As the time to go neared, I felt myself resisting. I didn't want to leave my cocoon of depression and go to a retreat where I would be made to spill my guts to complete strangers. I didn't want to do that. Not while I was feeling so vulnerable. I even told my husband on the way to the airport that I didn't want to go and continued to dig in my heels and resist even after I'd arrived.

The Pretend Mary didn't want to do this, and the Real Mary was pushing me beyond any fears I was having. I knew I couldn't continue on the depressive, self-destructive path I was on, and deep down, I wanted it so badly to stop. I also knew that I was the only one who could make that happen.

The first thing that hit me when I got off the plane was how good the warmth felt, having come from a dreary February in Seattle. A couple-hour bus ride later and we were at a quaint beach resort with a dozen open-aired casitas, one of which would be my home for the next week.

The first night was a meet-and-greet ice breaker and an overview of the retreat activities. I felt distant and disconnected, knowing everyone there paid big money to participate and were excited to do so, except me. I felt like the odd man out, though I didn't show it because now Pretend Mary was doing her thing, smiling and chit-chatting.

That night I went to bed thinking about the ladies I had just met; they all had goals and expectations for our week ahead. I thought about how I fit in, why I was there. I thought I was there for my niece and sister-in-law, but inside of me, I was there to find myself. I wanted to find the Real Mary.

I wanted to learn how to get the 5A's met by me. It's nice to get them from others, but to be truly happy, it has to come from the inside out.

While at this retreat, I journaled every day. Journaling helped me to process what I was experiencing and how it was affecting me. This part of my book is taken from those journal entries.

Vividly Woman Retreat in Troncones, MX

February 29, 2013

I am on a journey here in Mexico to try to rediscover Who I Am because I've been lost. I lost myself. Probably because of menopause (I don't know), but I feel like all my hormones drained from me and with it, my spirit, to the point that I feel totally empty. I've lost my happiness, my spirit, my joy, my passion. I feel like an empty, numb shell and I am so totally lost. Like my pilot light has gone out. I know that I am the only one that can re-light it, but I just can't find the matches. Because I can't figure it out, I have isolated myself from my husband, friends, and family —

everyone. I still go about "some kind of life," but I am just pretending to be me, to live, to be, because I really don't know who "me" is anymore.

This journey is a good starting point and has gotten me to slow down and really think about it and try to figure it out. I'm tired of being sad. I'm tired of my internal fight. I'm ready to open up and find my way back to the Real Me. I do know, deep in my heart, that I don't want to lose my husband and those I love in the process. I started thinking about my husband and how grateful I am for the good in him. He is supportive and has always been there for me. He is always consistent, and I know he truly cares about me and loves me by all the things he does. Even things I can't do for myself. He is very generous with himself. I appreciate him and all his gifts. I know I don't say it, but I feel it.

I mean these things from the deepest of my heart.

I've come to realize that I really am guarded with my true feelings and insecurities. It's safer for me to have short-term, less deep relationships with people because I don't know how to give deeply of myself. I never learned how because I have always been so needy. This "something" I will learn how to do, but I have to start by *loving myself. This I don't know how to do, but it is another thing I will learn. I am open and ready to learn. I know it will take work, and there will be struggles on this journey. I can do this.*

I have been reflecting a lot, the past intermingling with the present. I was never "good enough" growing up and have carried this "need to be perfect" with me throughout my life. I can't ever seem to get there because I judge myself: too fat, too thin, too this, too that, didn't/doesn't matter; I never seem to be right. So, I just go along – sometimes ignoring this feeling but mostly pretending. Where do I go from here?

I am still a vulnerable child, so afraid, so scared, so sensitive inside. This process I am going through will bust me open. Here, I am in a loving environment with women just like me. We all have the same issues and pain. And there is so much support to just bust out and let your vulnerability show.

March 1, 2013

On the second day, we began with A Birthing Experience (being birthed by moving through a grouping of rocks that resembled a birth canal simulating a rebirth).

As you moved through the rock birth canal on the beach, the other women were waiting with open arms on the other side to welcome you into the world. They were nurturing and loving. The entire group was there to hold each participant in their arms and hum to them. I chose to pass on this exercise. Why? Consciously, it was Day 2, and after all the crying I did on Day 1, I didn't want to cry again. That's what I told myself at the time. Now, thinking more about it, I did not feel I deserved to be held and nurtured. Maybe, when I was a child and wanted to be held and nurtured, I was disappointed when I didn't get it. I was afraid to be rocked, held, and hummed to for fear I would be disappointed. I know I was scared to do the activity. The fear of disappointment of childhood all came flooding back.

March 2, 2013

Today is my third day. I silently walked the beach for 30 minutes. I am walking to my death – the last 30 minutes of my life. I felt at peace and ready to go. I walked in turtle tracks, bird tracks, horse tracks, dog tracks, and people tracks. I knew I was just another creature trying to survive. Then my mind took a break, and the real me started working. My soul came alive. I realized that I needed to forgive. I knew this was a step I had to take. So, I wrote in the sand:

Mom, I forgive you.

My husband, I forgive you.

Forgive me.

Afterward, I was sharing this with my friend, and she said, "You didn't forgive yourself?"

"I know," I said, "I wasn't ready to, but I hope I will before the end of the retreat."

March 4, 2013

The activity for today was to draw a circle around yourself in the sand to represent your comfort zone. Interesting, mine was small. Is it because I am comfortable with people in my space? What does the circle signify? I will figure it out.

Each day, a little more of my layers get peeled away. I don't know if I will get to the core, but I will sure try. People have commented that they see my walls slowly coming down. I can feel this; I am lighter inside.

I have not yet surrendered myself; I can't quite let go, but I know when I do, it's going to be so releasing and joyous.

I will celebrate each slow step.

I realize that menopause may only play a small part in this. What's going on in my head – my thoughts – are what's eating me up alive and draining all my good energy. All my past beliefs are bubbling up.

March 5, 2013

On the fifth day, I am beginning with what I am grateful for. I've taken so much for granted. I am truly appreciative of:

My dear husband

Being able to breathe, walk, talk, experience, excellent health, all my senses

Roxy (my dog) brings me joy and unconditional love

My comfortable living conditions – a bed, warmth, food, money – all the essentials are there

Friends and family – those that care about me

THANK YOU, I AM GRATEFUL

I will try not to take anyone or anything for granted again. I will try to show my appreciation and to say how I feel to them instead of thinking it in my head. I will be true to myself and honest.

I have to really work hard at this because it is essential yet difficult for me to do.

The more I can show and voice love, the more positive energy I put out, the more will come back and fill the need in me so I can pass even more on. The idea of this makes me feel so hopeful and gives me direction toward my purpose.

There is so much love here. Hugging, crying, holding, laughing, touching, and more crying as we all let go of our pain.

I want to desperately break down my walls and surrender and be open. I pray that I can and will be able to carry this home with me – forever until I die.

Pass on the love that we all so desperately need. I am now ready to move through the birthing canal. Everyone is so happy for me. I stepped between the rocks and slowly eased through them. I'm coming into this world made of Pure Love. I feel alive and excited to be in this world. I am open to everything and so happy. I feel engulfed in arms of love. I am being rocked by so many arms. I feel the heartbeats. I hear the humming and feel the compassion and mothering. I am loved. I am open and moving forward. I am learning to trust. Now is the time for me to be sacred.

We are learning to harness our energy, through the breathing process/technique of harnessing that we just learned. I finally felt that I was okay, just the way I am. I am "good enough" just as I am. Boy, do I wish I had learned this sooner. Like when I was born. I need to practice this! I really feel blessed and full of life right at this moment. I will practice more loving action and words and fewer negative thoughts in my head!

March 6, 2013

Today is a big day. We went into the cave. We climbed up a mountain for about an hour, then sat in a circle at the mouth of the cave and had a group discussion about facing our shadows, what we were afraid to face. We then rappelled down into a deep, dark, and dangerous cave with ropes. Bats were flying; I had guano under my fingernails. There were stalactites and stalagmites everywhere.

When I got to the bottom, I found a dark corner, ready to face my fear. I sat for a long time, oblivious to anyone else while listening to the beat of a drum, relaxing in my corner, smelling and observing my environment, open to whatever came to me. I thought about everything – my childhood, this past week, how I feel, why I've been pretending, everything, my whole life hit me. I had my phone and started writing in my notepad. I wrote the following while there:

"All my life, I have not been good enough since I was a kid, so I created this person that people would like because I am so afraid of rejection. I never had a close friend except for my husband – my only friend. Then I retired and went into menopause. I slowly started withdrawing from my husband, people, life and becoming a recluse. Not knowing why I was doing this but knowing there was a reason I had to go through this deep sadness. In the cave, I realized my real demon was that I am not a real person; I am a fake I made up to please everyone so I would be liked. I never confronted or shared my real feelings and self. Because who would like her, she's not good enough? So my big fear now is WHO AM I? And where do I go from here?"

I broke open. I would continue to open up.

After climbing out of the cave (with rope burns and scrapes), I celebrated this momentous physical accomplishment and "ah-ha" moment.

Afterward, I talked to my niece and let her read what I wrote in the cave. She said, "Mary, you were so instrumental in helping me to grow and become the person I am. When we were living in Montana, and we would come to visit, you always took time for me and talked to me." She thanked me for valuing her as a person and talking to her without judgment, and letting her be herself. She was in her early teens at the time.

Wow! That changed my whole perspective. I started thinking about all the people I had an effect on. All the students I worked with over the years. One of which was Richard. I met Richard when he was 14 years old. He is now 45, and we have remained close, dear friends for 30 years. He has said the very same to me many times. He said I was the first person that ever talked to him like a real person and cared what he had to say.

I am comfortable talking to teenagers. I am myself, and I am real, at ease, and safe with them, without judgment. Yeah! So, the truth is, all along, I have been a real person. I work harder at applying that to adults (who I perceive to be more judgmental of me) and be safe like I am here at the retreat. I have to not judge myself in my head, either.

I will be me again!

March 7, 2013

I had a rough day today. I guess there are bumps along this journey. I am back in my head and stuck there – thinking. Once I decided to get involved and be a participant, my goal was to get back to the Mary I knew, which was the Pretend Mary. She was the Mary I was comfortable with, and I wanted her back. It dawned on me that I would never get her back. I would never be the same person again. At first, this realization made me feel sad and lost. I grieved this loss, and then fear bubbled up. I had no experience to draw on to anticipate where I was going. It was scary not knowing who I was going to be. This was all new.

This grief continued into the evening during our group meeting. Even though I am safe and not judged, I am feeling emotionally stuck and fragile. Tonight, people shared their deepest pain, and even though I can feel their pain, I didn't have the energy in me to offer them support. For some reason, I can only go to a certain point, and then I freeze and can't go any further emotionally. Maybe this is why I have never had a close friend or meaningful friendship. Why am I this way? My shield is up over my heart.

I look at their faces and their hearts, and as I hear each person's story, I deeply feel their pain. It is easy for me to absorb other's pain, but it is still difficult for me to share my own. I am still insecure and afraid to trust, but I am loving myself a little bit more to the point that I was able to write this.

In the morning, I woke up feeling sad and alone. I know I am not alone, but I can't seem to reach out and ask for what I need. I realize I am so insecure and afraid. I can only go so far, and then I freeze up emotionally, to the point that I physically need to getaway. I don't know why I stop myself from opening up to that deeper level. What am I so afraid of? Why can't I be more trusting?

I am a good acquaintance, a good helper, but hiding myself. I just can't let go of this insecurity – this feeling of "being a bother" when I see so much pain in others. I get so scared. I have no energy; I'm so drained. But I reminded myself of my Hope inside. And blindly, I continued on.

March 8, 2013

Today I found my JOY!! I have found my happiness!! I woke up in the morning, and there it was. I don't know where it came from, but I felt like dancing like a little kid, and I did. This was the first time in a long time (when I was in Iowa with my family) that I actually felt joyful and happy and loved. I am relieved to know that I still have it in me.

Feeling something inside makes me able to give of myself and open myself up to accept others.

I recognized that the little girl inside of me was allowed to be in charge. In trying to protect me, she created the Pretend Mary to help me survive. I've functioned this way for so long. I am tired; it's too much work.

Here in Mexico, I acknowledged her and faced her. I recognized her role in the past but that she needed to take a break and let the Real Mary take over. I appreciated all she did. She will now be a continual support because she only wants the best for me.

That was the last time I really saw the Pretend Mary. Once in a while, she'll test the waters and try to come out, but she knows she's not welcome and always disappears. She's no longer needed. I had looked through the window at myself as a child, and I saw this wounded child. I saw a baby in a crib desperate for Attention, "Mom, please notice me. I'm here, too." This need followed me most of my life.

When I finally got the Attention, I got it from my husband. What I didn't get was Acceptance and Allowing. Acceptance of who I was, the way I was. I thought he wanted to mold me into the wife and person he wanted. Once I found Real Mary, I needed him to Allow me to be — perfect just the way I am.

After eight days, I am leaving the retreat, these lovely women, and the serenity of Mexico. I am ready to practice the skills I learned and continue loving myself, working toward my joy, and being the real me. I am returning home to my life as a different person. I am not the same. This experience made me more than I had been before. It helped me to look into myself and grow. Grow in love.

When I finally stopped needing the 5A's from outside myself, I felt like I'd lost an old friend in Pretend Mary, and in a way, I did. Once I opened up to the Real Mary and observed, explored, and released my past misbeliefs from childhood that I carried into adulthood, I was able to move forward. Moving forward meant I could give myself the 5A's. I didn't need to get them from others. I realized I could give them to myself; I needed to give them to myself. With this realization came the pulling together of best practices to help me do just that. That's when I started to create my TMO Toolbox.

Moving forward meant I could give myself the 5A's. I didn't need to get them from others.

It wasn't my experiences in Mexico that saved my life. It was me. I was ready to make a change in my life, and the Mexico retreat was where I chose to give myself permission to make that change and to be the Real Mary. I know eventually, I would have accomplished this process of finding myself at home. Inside, I wanted to change, and I would by using the tools and skills I acquired and put in my TMO Toolbox. My rebirth could have happened anywhere at any time. It was up to me. It was always up to me, whenever and wherever I was ready. If I can do it, you can do it. Anyone can do it if you really desire to change.

Mexico is where my soul woke up, and my self-esteem did, too. I began to listen to my soul talk, dive into my inner self, look closely at myself for the first time, and start to love myself. My heart opened, and the healing began.

I believe that everything happens for a reason, in its own time. Every experience offers a gift. Mexico was my time, my gift. I was open to the Universe and willing to examine my past, my beliefs, and my misbeliefs. I was ready to be the Real Mary and let go of the Pretend Mary I had created and nurtured for 60 years for safety and security.

Once the door opens, you can't unopen it, nor would you want to. Once I became aware of the burden of Pretend Mary and the effort it took to maintain her, I slowly felt safe enough to let her go and found the Real Mary inside.

"You've always had the power, my dear; you just had to learn it for yourself."

– Glinda (The Good Witch),
The Wizard of Oz

About a month after my return from Mexico, I reached a breaking point.

I had been talking to my husband about something insignificant. I don't even remember what it was. The topic wasn't important. I remember feeling like I was through talking and didn't want to hear any more about it. I started walking away, heading upstairs. He was following me, continuing to talk. I reached the second-floor landing, and I turned and was looking down at him. He made a comment. It triggered something in me from my past. It was something that hit a raw nerve in me at the wrong time, or maybe it was the perfect time. I don't remember the words but they were an emotional trigger. I lost it. I lost all my senses. I couldn't see or hear. I saw a burst of light. I started screaming. I screamed at the top of my lungs – a primal scream. I was screaming and sobbing hysterically for 30 minutes.

I screamed over and over and over, "I quit! I quit! I quit! I quit! I quit!" I actually fell to the floor screaming and sobbing until my voice was hoarse, and I was completely empty, purged clean. There was no strength and nothing left to say. I got out of me what I desperately needed to release. I released the guilt, the shame, a lifetime of pain I carried. The burden was too much, and I couldn't carry it anymore. I didn't want to carry it, and it was an unnecessary burden I chose. I felt it throughout my entire body. I never looked at him. His person and his feelings at the time meant nothing. I couldn't tell you if he was even there.

My husband didn't know what hit him.

This was a release I needed desperately, or it wouldn't have happened. It was a part of my healing process. I learned courage, how to stand up for myself and fight for my beliefs, fight for me. I released my wounded child and let her come out of the closet and be Real Mary.

Another realization was he gave me the gift to not take things personally. If something is said about me or to me in a positive or negative way, it is my choice how I perceive it. I realize it's not about me; it's about the person saying it. I have to be true to myself, be sure of myself, and especially love myself.

I stopped allowing others to hurt me and owning their opinions.

When I finally gave up trying to live up to the expectations of others and love myself just the way I am, I felt free. I realized that no one was going to make me happy except myself. It had to come from the inside out. The more I accepted, forgave, and loved myself, the more I accepted, forgave, and loved others and allowed them to be who they were. They are just like me and are perfect just the way they are. We are all alike.

When I finally gave up trying to live up to the expectations of others and love myself just the way I am, I felt free. I realized that no one was going to make me happy except myself. It had to come from the inside out.

I was a people pleaser. I still try to make people happy, but now I do it in an empathetic, compassionate way as opposed to a pretender way.

The breaking point that day with my husband was about me and my healing. I was screaming for me, the Real Mary. I needed me. I needed time alone with myself. I was craving the real me. I wanted to meet me again and love me like I never had. I remembered who I am. "I quit" meant I was no longer the same person (the Pretend Mary), reacting the same way to the same words. I was no longer going to give away my power and accept what was being said, feel bad, stuff it in, and move on. I just wasn't going to take it from anyone. I realize that I didn't handle it the best way I could have by talking it out and speaking my truth. Unfortunately, my husband took the brunt of my lack of voice. I just let out all the built-up energy and frustrations I had stuffed throughout my entire life. I got it all out. I released it all. I felt new.

I immediately went to bed and slept for 12 hours, totally spent and empty. The next morning, he came to me and held me. We curled up in bed together, and I was able to talk about what had happened. I realized I gave my relationship with my husband its meaning coming from my past (Pretend Mary) instead of the present (Real Mary). Once I remembered who I really am, I was able to let go of my past misbeliefs and accept him for who he is and allow him to be. I stopped reacting and started accepting. I finally explained to him that I purged some of my past mis-beliefs, old baggage, and pain by dumping on him, which got triggered by words he used.

This was a tremendous turning point in my life. This was the point that I put myself first. I allowed myself to be most important over everyone else. I changed myself at that moment and have never looked back except to periodically see how far I've come.

I made my self-care my priority. I changed my thinking and opened up to me. I stopped allowing other people's opinions and judgments to have an effect on me. I stopped owning them, taking responsibility for them, and started simply allowing them to be.

I began to play more. I explored my city of Seattle. I acted like a tourist and wandered around in quirky shops, art galleries, music venues, ate ethnic food – I turned my senses on high. I went to see live musicals at the theater. I started playing miniature golf. I would go to the park and get on the swings or play on the jungle gym. I love to dance, and I took dance lessons. I started traveling. I visited family and friends. I started hiking in the mountains. I looked at what made me happy and started doing those things.

Ever since I first saw the Pacific Ocean, I have been drawn to its magnificence. I had spent years, on and off, living in beach towns. One day, I decided I wanted to buy a cottage at the beach. I called my husband and remember saying, "Honey, I bought a house." That was one of the boldest things I had ever done in our married lives, but I knew it was right. The minute I walked through the threshold of the beach house, I had an engulfing sense that I was supposed to live there. I knew this was my house, my retreat, my sanctuary. It spoke to me, and I fell in love with it. I even put in a dance floor where the little dining room was. Every time I go to my little beach house, I dance.

I became a puppy, young and alive. Everything was new and exciting. One day, as I was walking my puppy around my yard on her leash, somehow, she managed to wiggle out of her collar and was free. Oh, how she loves to run free. When I say free, I

mean running around with total joy. She ran huge
circles so fast all four paws actually left the ground,
and she looked like she was flying with her ears
suspended straight out. She jumped over flower
beds, and she rolled in the grass. She was happy. She
was living her true self, no cares, no worries, just
pure enjoyment. I felt joyful watching her. She
reminded me of myself when I finally took off my
self-imposed collar (the should's, the have-to's, the
expectations of others). So, of course, I had to run
around the yard with her, laughing as we played
together. It always feels so good to let loose and run
free.

As I ran, I felt an essence engulf me completely in
light. It was surrounding only me, like a bubble. I
knew I was experiencing something different and
very special. I felt like I was radiating love. I was so
overwhelmed with this all-encompassing love that I
started to cry tears of pure joy. I stopped running,
and it stopped. I started running again, and it came
back, more powerful than before. I started choking
up with loving tears and yelled, "Thank you! Thank
you!" I stayed with this feeling/experience for

several moments because I just had to have it. It was beyond words.

I have never felt this much pure love ever in my life. At that moment, I knew I had everything I needed inside of me. I was at peace and grateful.

Since then, as I go through my day, I remember that feeling and bring it into my awareness and remind myself that I am love and it's always in me.

I finally realized that all my blaming of my mother, my husband, my childhood, society, and any person who said something I considered a personal attack, was really myself holding me back. Even though none of them were with me throughout my life, I carried them with me; I heard the words, like old recordings in my head. It was my perception and my choice to carry my skewed version of statements and actions with me throughout my life. When I started to become aware of what I was saying to myself, I realized it was me doing this to me; no one was with me. It was all me. That was the moment I faced my pain, welcomed it in, and released it in a matter of seconds. The relief was immediate. The weight was lifted. I felt free for the first time in my life. Once that door opens, you cannot go back. What a relief when I woke up to the real me and said, "I quit."

When I started to become aware of what I was saying to myself, I realized it was me doing this to me; no one was with me.

It was all me.

I misbelieved:

- Everything they did, thought, or said was right to them. If you didn't think the way they did, you were wrong.

- There was no patience for people; if you didn't think the way they did, you were ignored, insulted, or dismissed.

- All love was conditional. Love was given when you were in agreement; you did things the way they would do them, you conformed to what they believed was right, appropriate, and correct.

I tried hard, and sometimes I got it right, but mostly I didn't. I was different. I was me, and I couldn't be someone else. I spent a lot of time wondering what was wrong with me, and as a result, not liking myself. I didn't even consider that my perception was skewed, molded by culture, media, society – others. I believed what I was expected to believe. I acted the way I was expected to act. I thought the way I was expected to think. I felt the way I was expected to feel. I didn't realize this until I decided to be the Real Mary.

When I did, my perceptions of the people in my life, my mother, my husband changed. I began to see them like me. They, too, had learned skewed perceptions; they too had expectations placed on them. We are One, doing the best we can at the time, each at a different point in our Story, at a different place in our journey. Now I have compassion, empathize, and respect them because I started to see everyone and everything differently through the eyes of the Real Mary. The outside world didn't change; my inside world changed.

I still hear certain words that were triggers before: "you need to," "you should," "why don't you." Now when I hear them, I don't take the words personally, I don't internalize them, and I don't own them. I hear them and accept them from the person saying them and allow the words to be said. I smile and say, "thank you," knowing they mean well, and choose to do what makes me happy.

I asked myself, "Mary, would you say these things to a friend, someone you cared about?" The answer was a resounding NO! That's when I knew I had to take control and change the messages I was giving myself.

I realized that it wasn't the real me being criticized, put down, made fun of. It was my behaviors. I learned to separate the two. I learned that I wasn't my behaviors; they could change. I was the real me inside, and I could choose how to internalize other people's perceived attacks.

The outside world didn't change;

my inside world changed.

Birth to 65 years old. Real Mary to Pretend Mary to remembering Real Mary, this is my Story, my Circle. My journey now continues with happiness,

YOUR STORY IS A CIRCLE

love, and joy. And I hope my Story becomes everyone's Story.

I wiggled out of my self-imposed collar and leash. If you are wearing a collar and a leash that you put on yourself because you feel that you have to pretend to be someone you're not like I did, I want you to know you can take it off anytime you want to. You take it off by deciding you want your happiness to come first. Just ask, what would make me happy? Be the puppy. Play and follow your heart. It's your choice. There is always hope.

I started my process of finding myself, the Real Mary, before going to the Retreat in Mexico. I worked with the few tools I found before going and the new tools I learned there, then I practiced the skills. I sensed and, deep down, knew that there was something more to life, to myself, and I wanted to find out what that was.

The experience I had in Mexico was a wake-up call for me, and it was the start of a new beginning, a new phase of my life. I said before, it was a bumpy road, and there were times when I slipped back into my old patterns, misbeliefs, and negative self-talk. I knew I had to help myself; I was the only one who could. It's like when you make a New Year's resolution to lose weight. You are serious, inspired, and determined to diet and exercise. After a month, you find you're not exercising anymore. One more month and you've started eating some ice cream and drinking soda pop. Soon you are back to your old habits. Why? Because it's easier.

So, when I noticed I was slipping back to my earlier default position, I went back to reading self-help books, like I started before going to Mexico. I read the work of many authors (noted at the beginning of the book). I surfed the internet for anything spiritual that could help me keep my momentum going and continue on my desired path. I talked to psychics and mediums. I knew, somehow, that what I was seeking was going to come in the spiritual realm. I had hope and sought out information. I continued to acquire skills, and they became my tools. They turned me on to happiness, love, and joy, which I nurture each day and often multiple times a day. I do this by practicing the tools in my TMO Toolbox. Five years later, I am still practicing, but now it comes easily and naturally.

And now, I'd like to introduce you to my TMO Toolbox. It is here to help you like it helps me to build the life you desire through awareness, creating new habits, practice, patience, and love.

CHAPTER 8
MARY'S TURN ME ON (TMO) TOOLBOX

In this section, I will introduce you to my Turn Me On (TMO) Toolbox, which will provide you with the tools you will need to bring about positive changes in your own life.

Are you living the life you want?

Are you living a life that makes you happy?

Are you living a life of love?

Are you giving yourself permission to live?

You are responsible for your happiness, peace, and well-being. You choose your attitude. You can always change something you don't like by changing your thoughts about it. You're the only one that gets to decide what you think. Your power belongs to you, keep it, cherish it, don't give it away. You have all the answers inside yourself. Trust yourself. You are human. You have free will. You are the master of your Story. You make mistakes, and it's okay. It's part of being human, so be gentle, loving, patient, and forgiving with yourself. You will get there.

To build a building, you need tools. To build a happy life, you need tools.

My Toolbox isn't a Craftsman, Kobalt, Stanley, or a Skil. This toolbox doesn't have drawers, tiers, latches, or cubby holes. I call it the "Turn Me On Toolbox" because that's what it does for me. It's the tools that woke me up and turned me on to the real me.

My Turn Me On Toolbox is filled with best practices from many different sources. These tools were not created by me. There are many hands at work here, and they are listed on my Acknowledgments page. I honor and share their knowledge and brilliance with you. I urge you to do as I did and read their amazing works.

The first step in building your TMO Toolbox is to realize your most powerful tools are your thoughts. No one can use them for you or stop you from using them. You are the only one in control of them.

Begin by loving yourself. This work must come first, and it must be a daily practice. The more you love yourself, the more you can share that love. When you practice these tools daily, they will become a part of you, part of your Story. They will reframe the way you think. As time goes on, you won't notice this happening; it will be automatic. You will notice that you are happier, filled with gratitude and love.

There is no priority to the order in which you use these tools. No one is more useful than another; any more than a hammer is more important than a screwdriver. They are equally useful but in different situations. They are easy to use and only require an inner desire. As you read through these tools and try them out, you can easily put together your own set of tools, skills, and practices that work for you. Then create your own Toolbox.

Today, pick one small thing that you would like to change about yourself that would raise your self-esteem and make you feel good, then commit to it every day. It doesn't have to be huge, just take one small thing from my TMO Toolbox and start creating your own TMO Toolbox.

A few examples are:

- Meditate
- Take 15 quiet minutes alone
- Go for a walk
- Spend time in nature
- Exercise 20 minutes every day
- Practice paying attention to your self-talk
- Practice being in the moment

Whatever change you want to make is fine. The most important thing is to get started. This change will shift your dynamics to a higher level of accountability, self-esteem, and self-empowerment.

Practice this change every day and it becomes a part of the new happy you. You won't even have to think about it; it will come naturally. And when you feel ready, pick another and continue practicing.

Your toolbox can help you slowly take down your shield and open your heart to Love. You can be happy, full of love for yourself and every living thing. You can live in the moment and enjoy life. It can help you see that your main purpose in life is soul growth, remembering who you are, experiencing, learning, gifts/lessons, loving all, and passing on your gifts. How you fulfill this is unique to you. It is a result of your free will, which represents you and guides you to your purpose. You are a spiritual being living a human experience.

You can't teach happiness, love, joy, and goodness in a classroom, read about it in a book, or find it on the internet. It has to be discovered within the depths of your heart when you are finally ready to go looking for it. I found it to be a lifetime process of confronting my own weaknesses, misbeliefs, and past. It's a process that has no end. It is your ongoing journey, your Story, your Circle. To do this requires practice, daily practice, sometimes hourly, so we all need tools to practice.

You can't teach happiness, love, joy, and goodness in a classroom, read about it in a book, or find it on the internet. It has to be discovered within the depths of your heart when you are finally ready to go looking for it.

Use these tools when you slip backward, when you feel out of balance, when your ego runs amok, when you can't feel your happiness, when you need to make a decision or choice, when you need to say something important to someone, when you face a challenge, when your needs aren't being met, or when you feel lost, empty, or you simply get stuck. In those moments, remind yourself of the assortment of wonderful tools you have to amend, fix, change, and guide you through any situation.

Don't be afraid to mix and match your tools. Every situation requires a different combination of tools. Even now, sometimes I can do it skillfully, and sometimes it's a bumpy road of trial and error. Sometimes I have to sharpen something, clean the rust off, or decide if it's a flathead or Phillip's screwdriver that's needed or both. It will be the same for you. As long as you trust in the tools, you will find the path that works for you.

It's okay to make mistakes in an effort to improve yourself. I did! Give yourself permission to make mistakes.

To use any tools properly, to get the best result from your tools, you must PRACTICE using them. You must feel them, work with them, and try them out in many different situations. PRACTICE, PRACTICE, PRACTICE! You can learn skills, but you'll never realize your full potential unless you put them to use. By practicing, you can learn to pick the most appropriate tool for your purpose and how to properly use that tool to get your most fulfilling results.

BUILD YOUR TOOLBOX

Now it's time to learn about the tools that will go into your toolbox. As you build yours, remember that there is no one recipe for being happy. We are all different, so as you familiarize yourself with the tools below, feel free to experiment with life's experiences and find what works for you.

Living in the Present Moment with Hope

When you tune into your awareness, in the moment, the small voice (your heart/gut/intuition) that speaks from your soul gives you clarity. You will always know the right direction to go or not go, and you will no longer worry, have indecision, fear of the unknown, past regrets, or beat up on yourself. Listen to your intuition; allow it to guide you.

To tune in, say to yourself, "I am alive in my breath; I am at ease in my heart. I don't need to go anywhere else to find peace. I am already home. I always have Love in my heart and Hope in my life."

Hope is activated in the present moment. Present moment awareness is the now, without the mind analyzing or judging. You can say these words or create your own. Whatever words you use can be said silently in a quiet place, in your office, or out loud while driving in your car. It is important that you feel them and believe them.

When you're in the present moment, you can let everything pass through you as if you were invisible. Don't resist. It's as if there is no one to get hurt. When someone says or does something hurtful to you, or there is something irritating going on outside or around you, like slow traffic, you're running late, or there is something that could interfere with your peace and happiness, envision it moving past you.

Live in the here and now – the present moment. Memories of the past are a part of your life that can be happy or sad. They are your life experiences and a part of your Story. But memory lane is not a place to live your life. Let go of the past, learn from it, move on, and don't relive it. Let go with love and forgiveness. It can no longer touch you.

Living in the future is a place that may never come. By waiting for the unknown, you are missing what is happening right now. Living in the past and future is a main cause of unhappiness, pain, and lack. Why do we do it? Because deep down, we're afraid that happiness is somewhere else, when all along, happiness is always inside of us, right here right now. We muddy it up with negative thoughts and feelings.

You are not your thoughts (ego); the Real you is the observer of those thoughts (awareness). That voice in your head is your false self, the one that worries, sabotages, judges, regrets, and is afraid.

Throughout your day, try to catch the chatter in your head, listen to your gut, and pay attention to what you're thinking about, how you feel. Know if you miss out on the present, you will miss out on living life. In the moment, scan the space you're in and focus on individual items. If you're in a room focus on the lamp, the chair, a pencil, the ceiling, even the end of your nose; or if you're outside, a leaf, a cloud, a grain of sand. Like all skills, it takes daily practice to develop. A little practice and reminders every day, and it becomes a part of you.

Stop and Take a Deep Breath

The secret to slowing time down, being in the moment, and in your inner space one with Creator is to focus on your breathing. Breathing is an involuntary bodily function that you don't have to think about, but when you mindfully pay attention to your breath and breathe deeply, it slows the heart rate, lowers the blood pressure, relaxes muscles, and releases tension. Practice taking deep belly breaths. "Deep breathing counters the effects of stress by slowing the heart rate and lowering blood pressure," says psychologist Judith Tutin.

Practice deep breathing from your belly to the top of your head. Slowly inhale, filling your belly, your chest, your throat, and your head with a deep inhale of breath. Hold it in for several seconds, then slowly release it. Do this a few times, at least three.

Are you anxious at work about an upcoming meeting or a deadline? Are you wound up about not being able to clean your house or finish chores? Are you worrying about unpaid bills? Do you feel like there's never enough time? Are you apprehensive about a new relationship?

When you're caught up in the busyness of your day, notice this, and stop right where you are and refocus your mind and heart on your breath. With each deep breath you take in, imagine every cell of your body being filled with love. With each breath out, imagine your stress going out with it. Pay attention to taking that deep breath in and letting it out. Slowly follow your breath in and slowly follow your breath out. Then try to pay attention to the space between each breath.

Be aware that your breath has a purpose. Be aware that each cell of your body has a purpose, and each cell is working in harmony with your entire body through your breath. Inhaling...exhaling.

Throughout your day, take time to notice your breath. It reminds you that you are alive, right here, right now. Breathe in life.

Our breath fuels us in so many ways. When you feel like a hamster running on its wheel, it is time to stop and tune out the voices in your head, those thoughts. You are bigger than that. Just breathe.

Be aware of each deep breath you take. Your heartbeat slows, your mind calms, and your body relaxes. Breathe in peace, and exhale stress. Breathe in love, compassion, strength, and peace deep into yourself. As you exhale, let go of tension, limitations, distractions, and things beyond your control.

Tell the Truth

Your path to freedom begins with telling the truth. As you begin your journey, it's important to be honest and tell the truth to everyone about everything. Be honest with yourself. Once you learn to be honest with yourself about your feelings, you are able to be honest with everyone you know and everyone you meet. It's healthy for you to tell the truth about yourself and about everything in every situation, with others and yourself. You will avoid misunderstandings, hurt feelings, and acting with passive-aggressiveness when you do.

Your feelings never lie. If you, your spouse, or your friend has trouble telling the truth, then look to the feelings being presented. That's where the truth is. Try to look past the lie and try to focus on the feelings behind it. Usually, the motive behind lying is to not hurt someone else's feelings. Try to be truthful but don't beat up on yourself if you slip up.

This may not be easy because you may realize you tell white lies and fibs like they were the truth, and you may even believe them. Once you start to tell the truth and be honest, from that point forward, you make a commitment to God. You can't go back into the past and correct anything. Be grateful for your past because it has helped make you who you are today. Choose not to live there. Take each moment at a time and approach it with truth, love, and by being the best person you can be.

Risk is Essential to Your Story

Learning to know yourself requires you to take some risks. You will be faced with lessons that will challenge you. Believe that everything (good and bad) happens for a reason; it's supposed to happen and happens when it is supposed to. There are no coincidences, and nothing happens "by accident." Remind yourself when faced with a situation that you are supposed to go through or an experience you're supposed to have that it wouldn't be happening unless there was something in it for you to learn. It's an opportunity to deal with a misbelief or to alter an old pattern. It comes when you are ready for it and can handle it and can learn from it. It has come to heal you in some way. It may also be an opportunity to help someone else. You may be in a position to inspire, guide, or heal another.

Look at your relationships and experiences and ask yourself some questions, "Why are these people in my life? What does each relationship have to teach me? What lessons am I supposed to learn from each of my life situations? Why did this happen to me?

Why did I have to go through the things I've gone through?"

We choose our soul experiences to receive a gift or lesson for our soul to evolve. Earth is our "school" for soul gifts and lessons.

I chose my mom. I chose my husband. I am continuing to choose people in my life. I'm continuing to choose my life experiences. With these many choices comes some risk. This is all a part of my Story, my Circle.

Know that you choose your lessons and gifts to learn and which you want to pass on to others in this part of your Story, this segment of your Circle. You came here to evolve your soul through lessons, gifts, and to share. That's why you are here. That's why we all have challenges. Our early years groom us for them. It's the perfect setting for what we need to experience to learn what we came here for.

Maybe in your Story, you've been physically abused or experienced death and grief, and from those things, you've learned forgiveness and acceptance. Maybe your Story of addiction has taught you strength and courage. Maybe your Story was that you had wealth but not happiness; you had to learn compassion. Maybe your Story is to be made fun of to learn to accept criticism. Maybe your Story is to work with people that irritate you, and you are here to learn tolerance and patience. That's why life here on earth is a bumpy road. The bumpy road is a good thing. There are ups and downs to learning. Life lessons come by learning to cope with the bumpy road.

What is your Story? What choices are you making? Stop and think about yours. You don't want to be like one of those kids in their senior year of high school that don't complete a course and has to come back to finish it up. You want to learn your lessons in this lifetime.

When someone enters your life unexpectedly, look for the gift that person has come to receive from you, and in so doing, you receive a gift. When you're struggling with a difficult situation, ask yourself, "What is the Gift? What is my highest choice? What is the lesson? What would Love do?" You are made of Love, and the only way to approach any person or situation is from your real self. Then make your choice. Try to view all situations, experiences, and things that happen as opportunities to help you make your choice. You teach what you have to learn. This holds equally true for any joyous experiences, happy moments, and blessings; they also happen for a reason, so appreciate them, even the little ones, and find the gift or lesson in it.

Try to view all situations, experiences, and things that happen as opportunities to help you make your choice.

Ask yourself, "Where in my life am I attaching my happiness to an outcome?" Can I shift my perspective to recognize the gifts of the journey? Can I be grateful for those gifts even if I don't "succeed?"

When you are stuck, know that Source will give you a push, guide you, and motivate your soul to grow. Think about the decision you have to make, then check with your gut and heart; it will never lie to you. If your gut feels calm, then the choice is right. If it feels upset, then the choice is not right. Then, let go. Just stop for a time. Shift from striving to believing, knowing that answers will come. Give thanks in advance. Wait. Listen. Receive. Know that everything always works out. Say THANK YOU to Source for guiding you to your best self.

From A Course in Miracles:

"No one is here is by accident, and chance plays no part in God's plan."

M-9.1:3

Eliminate Judgments

Try to remember the difference between judgment and observation, to see things as they are. Each of us is here to find our purpose and live our journey. You are not here to judge the journey of another's soul or how they live their life. You are here to be the real you, the best you that you can be. So, don't judge others. And if you are judged, know it's never about you; it's always about the person doing the judging. All judgment is really self-judgment. Their insecurities and fears come out as an attack, an insult, or blame. An attack is a cry for help.

Don't allow others to affect your happiness and how you feel about yourself, or let your joy depend upon what anybody else is living and doing. It's about what makes you feel good and focusing on that as long as it makes you happy. You get to choose your thoughts. You can't control circumstances or others, but you can control your thoughts and feelings.

Don't allow others to affect your happiness and how you feel about yourself, or let your joy depend upon what anybody else is living and doing.

Your happiness comes from the inside out. Reacting as hurt to what another is saying or doing is a choice you make. Start by admitting honestly to yourself exactly how you are feeling. Honor your honest feelings. Now honor that person judging because you don't know what they've been through; you haven't walked in their shoes. You haven't lived their Story, past experiences, or their day-to-day journey. You can only take care of yourself. Your journey is yours alone. Eliminate judging others.

Those who attack do not know they are blessed. They attack because they believe they are deprived. From *A Course in Miracles* (ACIM): T-7.VII.7:5-6.

When you judge, you want to be right, and you want someone else to be wrong. It separates us instead of bringing us together. Being thankful, caring, and compassionate brings us together. Helping someone rather than beating them up no matter what they have done is healing. Then forgive. It frees you from resentment, anger, and fear.

When you stop judging others, you stop judging yourself. Be compassionate to yourself and others. Judging yourself or others is learned. You weren't born being critical of your looks or someone else's body. The need to criticize is your own longing for the 5A's, and none can be obtained through criticism.

The need to criticize is your own longing for
the 5A's, and none can be obtained
through criticism.

Being judgmental can be unlearned. So wish them well on their journey instead of internalizing a hurtful remark or judgment. Fear and guilt are your enemies; love and awareness are your friends. Know you are here for your own love and happiness, so choose to forgive, love, and surround yourself with uplifting people. To have a loving relationship with another, you must have one with yourself. Start with yourself. You have to come first in order to draw the love you want into your life. This is how each of us can pass the goodness on in this world, one person at a time.

Love and Fear

Know that there are only two emotions – love and fear. One feels good, and one feels bad. Everything we do, think, or feel is based on these two emotions. What does your free will choose?

Love (happiness, joy, peace, contentment, kindness, gratitude, inspiration, hope, compassion, to name a few). Fear (guilt, jealousy, anger, frustration, apathy, anxiety, sadness, despair, to name a few). People get mad because they are afraid. The beliefs behind fear are anger, resentment, being a victim, and revenge. To change these beliefs, you must look in the mirror and really see yourself. Become aware of the beliefs you are carrying and no longer want. Focus on one at a time and examine it, where it started, why you keep it, and why you continue to feed and carry it. Ask yourself if it is true and if it is serving you or hurting you. Once you clearly see it as not true, change it, release it, and replace it with a positive belief, one that serves and uplifts you.

The Laws are very simple.

1. Thought is creative.
2. Fear attracts like energy.
3. Love is all there is.

Love is giving, sharing, and opening you up. It expands and continues growing in more love, and you want the love to continue because it feels good.

Unfortunately, from childhood, we've been taught fear from our parents, culture, and society. It's our default emotion. Begin to see that there is no bad; there is nothing to fear.

Were you conditioned to believe that the only way to be happy was to follow the rules and expectations laid out by your parents and society? Realize that happiness doesn't come from the outside world; it comes from inside of you. You were born with it. How happy would you be if you chose love from the inside out? How happy would you be if you chose love as your default emotion?

No one ever taught me that my thoughts become things.

No one ever taught me that I could be and have anything I want.

No one ever taught me that I was in charge of myself through my thoughts.

No one ever taught me that I have a built-in guidance system of feelings that monitors and guides me with my thoughts to always be able to feel good.

The power is in me. I taught myself by research-ing the Spiritualists I noted at the beginning of my book. And now, this is the path I am on. You can teach yourself, too. Love is what I think about in every situation, in every moment of the day. Bring Love to every situation. Ask yourself, "What would Love want? What would Love do?" Open yourself to the presence of love within you. When you focus on the love that you are, you can pass the love to everyone, and it comes back to you. Practice constantly and consistently remind yourself because we often still carry the fear reaction.

It's easy to get lost in the "Why is this happening to me? What's wrong with me? What did I do wrong?" Then you start to beat up on yourself. Try to catch yourself when you start to do this and remind yourself to go to love, to open your heart to love, and know that every part of Source loves you. Remind yourself that you came from Pure Love, and that is what you are made of. Listen to your gut, your inner voice. Keep your focus there and review the situation you are faced with. By choosing to have love in your heart, nothing else matters. Everything will always be well and work out. What you give to life returns to you.

"Use your heart to love somebody. And if
your heart is big enough, use your heart to
love everybody."

– Stevie Wonder

Daily Inspirational Emails

No matter if you're having a good day or a bad
day, a positive message can lift your spirits and
inspire you. I like to begin each day with a daily
inspirational message from my favorite sources:

- Daily Word from Unity -
  www.dailyword.com
- Daily Quote from Abraham-Hicks
  Publications - www.abrahamhicks.com
- TUT - A Note from the Universe -
  www.tut.com
- Daily Messages from Robert Holden -
  www.robertholden.com
- Hay House - www.hayhouse.com
- Eckhart Tolle - www.eckharttolle.com
- Conversations with God Foundation from
  Neale Donald Walsch - www.cwg.org
- Year of Healing from Amit Sood –
  www.resilientoption.com

Practice Gratitude

Love is the way you walk in gratitude. Practice gratitude and appreciate what you have. Practice gratitude because you can't have your attention on ego and gratitude at the same time.

Practice gratitude because you can't have your attention on ego and gratitude at the same time.

Thank Source, God, Universe, Divine Life, Creator for the day. Every morning, as soon as you are aware of being awake, think of something you are grateful for. I say, "Thank you for this day" because I am grateful I woke up and am breathing. Before you start thinking about the busyness of your day and your "to-do" list, think about what you are grateful for. Maybe it's your health, your spouse, your kids, your job, your five senses, or your warm and comfortable bed. Even before you get out of bed, give yourself time for gratitude, feeling good, what makes you happy, so you can start your day with positive energy.

Do the exact same thing at night right before you close your eyes and go to sleep. I say, "Thank you for this day." Then I relive my day and think of all the things that happened and the people that were a part of it, and I thank them. Try doing this every day. It will change you.

As you continue preparing for your day, give yourself some inspiration. You might say to yourself, "I am reborn. I adore me. I want to feel good. Nothing is more important than I feel good. I am free. I am happy! I want to be uplifted! I want to be happy and growing! I'm being guided by my inner being to what I want, and I WANT TO FEEL GOOD! I intend to be excited and happy about this day! I TAKE A DEEP BREATH! I say YES, YES, YES to life! I remind myself that my life is a gift, and I came here to live happily ever after. Use your own words, those that have meaning and motivation for you.

You can be grateful for anything in the moment. Get specific: a bottle of water, the smell of coffee, the people in my life, my health, the air that I breathe,

the peace my meditation practice gives me, my senses, my dinner, my toilet, my quality of life, even the hardships in my life and situations and people because they all teach me something for which I are grateful.

The more grateful you are, the more present you become and the more you are out of your ego. Gratitude amplifies the positive things, people, and experiences in your life and reminds you that you are truly blessed. Set your ego aside and give it a rest.

Think about how hard some people have it, their struggles – poverty, abuse, neglect, illness, physical pain, eminent death – you may realize that you have nothing to cry about. Remind yourself of the things you have to be grateful for. Every one of us, no matter our life situation, can always offer love.

No matter what the challenge is, no matter what the life event, if you are struggling, suffering, or filled with joy, try practicing gratitude. Find the blessing in the situation, find the gift in the challenge, find the love in the experience.

"It takes great learning to understand that all
things, events, encounters, and circumstances
are helpful." ~ ACIM Teacher's Manual

With this in mind, try to see all change as good; even if you don't see the gift at the moment, know it will come because everything always works out.

If you look at a challenge closely enough and try to understand why it causes you pain, you can find the gift. Challenges are the Source's way of showing you how strong you really are. You are always stronger than any problem. Thank Source for bringing you this problem, this pain, so you can acknowledge it and heal from it. Then move on.

If you look at a challenge closely enough
and try to understand why it causes you
pain, you can find the gift.

Focus on what you appreciate when you're struggling or suffering. What are you grateful for?

Every time you attach gratitude to an experience, you're training your mind. In future experiences, your mind will remember that goodness of gratitude and draw on it, again and again; you stop becoming the victim, your suffering and struggling ends, and your challenges become gifts.

Practicing gratitude can turn a bad thing into a good thing. When you look at the things you do every day as a joy, that's what they become. Parenting, going to your job, running errands, doing chores, going to meetings can each be viewed as a gift if you refocus and make that your choice. Choosing to find the goodness in every activity will bring you that goodness.

How do you practice gratitude? Are you as uplifting as you can be with everyone you meet? Do you smile and spread love and happiness? You can always give of yourself. Giving of yourself is easy.

Practice Forgiveness

A good definition of forgiveness comes from Oprah Winfrey: "Giving up the hope that the past could have been any different." Letting go of the past you thought you wanted and didn't have is an essential part of forgiveness. Forgiveness sets you free.

Forgive yourself and others for things said and done or not said and done. When you perceive someone has hurt you, look deeper at that person and see the frightened child and forgive them. Know that we all do the best we can. Forgiveness opens our hearts to self-love.

If you feel someone has wronged or hurt you, instead of being angry, resentful, or revengeful and wishing them pain, forgive them because they are already in pain, or they wouldn't have done what they did. What is said or done is always a reflection of the person doing it. They are hurt inside and give out pain in hopes that it will make them feel better. We do it, too. And if you look closely at yourself when you do this, you will see that there is some sadness, guilt, shame, insecurity, jealousy, or some other inner pain that you are trying to get relief from. Unfortunately, causing pain to others never gives you relief. For example, if you laugh at someone or call them stupid when they make a mistake, you quickly realize doing this doesn't make you feel any better, and more often than not, you feel worse. Instead, send them healing and loving thoughts. These thoughts will make you feel better and bring you some peace. The same is true when you forgive yourself for something you regret doing, even from your past. You can't change it. Reliving it only eats you up. Give yourself some peace and self-love by being gentle with yourself and letting it go, forgiving yourself, and learning from it. It is a process.

From David Simon, The Ten Commitments:

"Transforming judgment into understanding allows peace to replace hostility.

Understanding fosters forgiveness, which dissolves anger and fertilizes hope. This is the foundation of emotional freedom."

Forgiveness releases you from the one who hurt you or from your past. It's a choice you can make. Forgiveness is a skill that requires practice.

As you continue to practice forgiveness, some phrases you can use are:

- I forgive myself for the times I got angry, upset, frustrated, and beat up on myself.
- I forgive myself for being human.
- I forgive myself for forgetting that I am love.
- Forgiveness is a choice I make.
- Forgiveness is a gift I give to myself.
- I choose to let go of my past.
- I turn judgments into understanding.
- I am perfect just the way I am.
- There is nothing to forgive.
- When I accept "what is" every moment is the best moment.
- Say Thank You ♡ Say Thank You
- Forgiveness is my teacher; it carries me to happiness with love.

Positive Self-Talk

Words are powerful. They come out of your head and into the world, or they stay in your head and are meant for yourself. You are constantly talking to yourself, whether you are aware of it or not. Start to be more aware of the voice in your head and listen to it. Is it giving you positive or negative messages? Is it building you up or tearing you down? If your self-talk is more positive, then you will attract the positive aspects of life to you. If that little voice in your head is more negative, then negativity is what you will attract. Practice turning negative thoughts into positive thoughts. Catch the negatives when they start. When you first become aware that you have negative thoughts or behaviors, try to catch yourself as you are doing this and identify what the pattern is and at what moment you lost it. This is when you need to come up with a new positive thought or behavior. Then practice.

When you first become aware that you have negative thoughts or behaviors, try to catch yourself as you are doing this and identify what the pattern is and at what moment you lost it.

This is a skill. It requires practice at being aware. Be aware of your voice inside. Listen to it and choose your words so that they are uplifting and positive. Ask yourself, "Would I treat someone else the way I am treating myself, or would I say the things to someone else that I am saying to myself?" You can change the way you talk to yourself. Practice thoughts that bring you joy.

Self-Care Activity

Is there a challenge in your life right now? Is it causing your stress or anxiety? Think about it. Allow your mind and body to feel the emotions that arise. What emotions are you feeling? Spend some time with those feelings. Your emotions are communications from your soul.

Now remind yourself:

This is happening right now; these feelings will not last forever; they are temporary.

This is a bump in the road of my journey.

This is part of my Story.

Now wrap your arms around yourself and give yourself a big hug. Feel the love and comfort from yourself and all Source Energy flowing through your arms. You are so loved, and you are not alone.

Stop, slow down, breathe, go inside!
Let go of Negativity. Cultivate Love. All I seek
is within me.

Daily Affirmations

Daily affirmations can help you stay centered, no matter what you are facing. Positive affirmations can change the way you think in a short period of time. We are always thinking and listening to our inner voice. Sometimes the things you say to yourself aren't kind or helpful, like old thought patterns from childhood: "I'm not good enough. I'm stupid. I'm _____." These words hurt you. But using positive affirmations can turn those around.

The word affirmation means to make firm, so create what you want. When practicing affirmations, always use "I am" or "I choose" statements in thought, word, and deed. Rather than "I want more success and money" or "I want to be happy" use "I am successful and wealthy" or "I have money" or "I choose happiness" or "I have a happy life" or "Thank you Source for my successful life" or "I am grateful, Universe, for my healthy body."

Focus on the present tense as if it's already true. Affirmations only work when they are statements of something you already know or believe to be true. The power is in your thoughts and actions. What you think about becomes your experience. And your soul does not recognize "no" and "don't want." So, keep your thoughts focused on what you do want.

Affirmations only work when they are statements of something you already know or believe to be true.

Give thanks in advance for your desires, choices, and results. Believe it. What you call forth is what you think, feel, and say. So, if you say I want to be happy, you will receive the feeling of wanting. If you say I am happy, you will receive the feeling of being happy.

Affirmations can change as you change. Affirm the good stuff that means something to you. Make it personal.

You can easily implement daily affirmations into your life. Surround yourself with them. Find some favorites and put them on the lock screen of your phone or on your phone's calendar to pop up and remind you throughout the day. Print and frame one and hang it in your bedroom, a sticky note on your bathroom mirror, or your meditation spot.

Some ideas are:

- I open myself to the presence of love within me♡

- I am love, and a giver of love

- Let my breath be grace♡

- I Choose Happiness!

- Everything always goes right for me.

- Thank You for everything♡

- I am Grateful♡

- I'm perfect just the way I am.

- I love myself.

- I love, accept, forgive me.

- I'm inspired! I'm unstoppable!

- I am strong & courageous!

- I am doing the best that I can in this moment.

- The power is in me!

- I am good enough just as I am.

- I am worthy♡

- I deserve to be happy♡

- I will help one person feel worthy today.

Balance

Having balance in all aspects of your life is not only important but crucial – physically (body), emotionally (mind), and spiritually (soul). Balance in you can provide you with a long and healthy life. Strive to maintain daily balance in all areas of your life and to get good sleep, nourishing foods, and daily physical and mental exercise. Find something to get excited about, something that stimulates a passion in you. This can be at work, at home, or in your community.

Try not to get too distracted by all your "To Do" lists and timelines. Take time for yourself. Settle into stillness throughout your day and be the real you, the soul of you. By quieting the busyness in your head, you bring a centering calm to your mind and body, and then you can continue with your activities refreshed, renewed, and filled with gratitude.

Settle into stillness throughout your day and
be the real you, the soul of you.

To take time to quiet your mind with stillness, you do not need to sit for very long; whatever you can handle before your chatter mind starts invading your awareness. And it will. So focus on your breathing. This is not meditation or mindfulness. This is simply quieting your mind in stillness and balance. It takes dedication and practice to go inward and find your way to peace, calmness, and quieting your mind. Learn to stop and give your mind and body a break by giving them permission to relax, rest, and balance. When you take this time for inner balance and calming yourself down, you care for your physical and mental self and grow personally and spiritually.

Meditation

Research suggests that daily meditation may alter the brain's neural pathways and aid you with better sleep, lessen stress/anxiety/depression, improve your immune system, provide more oxygen flow in your body, and lower blood pressure and cholesterol. Meditation is a journey from external activity to inner silence. This simple practice provides a time of quiet reflection where you are one with God and open to inspiration. It's a time to rest your thoughts. Rest heals your body and awakens you spiritually, opening you to be receptive to spiritual messages. Being still every day leads you to more peace, more happiness, and more love in your life. Listening to the real you, your inner spirit, your soul connects you to all living things. It's a joyful awakening.

Where do you start? Start by listening for free on YouTube or downloading any of the free phone apps. You choose what helps you center yourself: certain music, the sound of a certain voice, how it makes you feel, guided or free-flowing. My preference is partly guided. I like Deepak Chopra's

Meditations, Abraham's Meditations, Joe Dispenza's guided Meditations, iRest Nidra Meditations, walking meditations, and sitting quietly by myself. There are so many to choose from. Try them on for size.

You can listen and meditate while sitting on the floor, sitting in a comfy chair, walking, or, my personal preference, lying down. You can use earbuds if that works for you. As long as you have a quiet place that is free of distractions, you can meditate. Tune out your surroundings and focus on your breathing. With each breath in and out, your heart rate steadies, your oxygen level rises. Fill yourself with peace.

Before starting, get comfortable and take a few deep breaths. Then start and focus on your breathing, a mantra, counting, or whatever will help you stay out of your thinking mind and in the present moment. Yes, your mind will wander and when it does, try to bring it back by focusing on your breath going in and out or the guidance of the meditation. You can meditate for 5 minutes to 45 minutes, depending on what you want to do that day, but make an effort to do it every day. Any time of day will do, whenever you have quiet time for yourself. First thing in the morning or last thing at night are good times. Meditation's healing properties can build up energy in you. Know that these moments will benefit you physically, mentally, and spiritually.

Afterward, you can lay there and thank Source, reflect, and pray.

You will feel refreshed and renewed, ready to face whatever comes to you.

Stimulate Your Senses with Music and Dance

Music can be a daily practice for you. You can easily create several playlists for your phone to meet different needs. My favorite "go-to" songs for uplifting are, *Thank You For This Day* by Karen Drucker, *I Wanna Thank You* by Mavis Staples, *I Hope You're Happy* by Blue October, *I Believe I Can Fly* by R. Kelly, and *I Hope You Dance* by Gladys Knight.

If you love to dance and move your body, get up and dance anytime, anyplace, even while you are walking. Just get silly and let your body move and flow in any way that feels good. Add a sense of humor to this fun. Crank the music up, flail your arms around, and move all over the place. If you love to dance, then dance. Don't wait. Do what makes you happy NOW!

Walking

Walking is a very healthy form of exercise, and meditating while you walk turns the whole experience into a super-healthy event for the body, mind, and soul. It encourages mindfulness, and it will help you to find peace of mind. It will lift your spirits, stimulate your brain, maintain balance, and a healthy weight. Walking meditation can be done anywhere: on your way to lunch during a break from work, on a busy city street, or in the middle of a shopping mall, on a wooded trail, or in a park on a weekend.

There are many good websites on the internet on beginning walking meditation. Here are some guidelines I've found, modified, and that I use in my daily practice.

If you are new to walking meditation, you may want to start in your own yard or a place that is comfortable and safe for you. Any location will work. Walking on a nature trail is ideal. Try starting out with 5-10 minutes. There is no time requirement, whatever works for you. Start by walking slowly, moving steady and evenly so you can be in the moment. Walk with your back straight, a smile on your face, and love and gratitude in your heart.

Before you start moving, prepare your body and mind for meditating on your walk. Feel all parts of your body, from your head to your feet. Relax each part and let go of any tension. One way is to take a deep breath; as you exhale, feel all the muscles in your body relax and then pay attention to your breathing, in and out. Do a few gentle stretches with each part of your body, then relax each part. Before you start walking, you can say, "On my walk today, I am open to nature and to all Source Energy. I open my mind, my body, and my soul. I am filled with love and happiness. I am energized. I walk in love."

Begin walking at your natural pace, whatever is comfortable for you. Focus your attention on the rhythm of your steps and your breath – left foot – right foot – left foot – right foot – breathe in – breathe out, letting the rhythm of your breathing soothe you. Feel the rhythm of your legs moving, feet touching the ground, arms swinging – your body moving. Try to let go of thoughts as they arise and focus your attention on the experience of walking. Notice how the body feels as you walk. Notice your feet touching the ground.

Breathe in the energy from the trees, grass and plants, people, and animals. Breathe in the energy from all living things around you. Feel it, smell it, taste it, hear it, and see it as it envelopes you. Feel this energy wrapping you up in love. Let it surround you and support you.

Meditate as you walk by focusing your attention again on your footsteps. Count your steps as each foot touches the ground, one, two, three, four, one, two, three, four, one, two, three, four. Or you can meditate by focusing on your breath, inhale, exhale, inhale, exhale, inhale, exhale. Follow the rhythm of it. I like to breathe in the word "thank" and breathe out the word "you."

Turn your attention now to your surroundings. Notice everything around you, the surface you are walking on, what you see, what you feel, the temperature, the colors, any sounds, and smells. Enjoy everything on this relaxing walk.

For a few moments, can you see your body walking and then step out of the body and be aware of yourself walking? Try to experience this awareness and be the real you.

Enjoy this relaxing walk for as long as you wish, feeling the refreshing and invigorating energy. When I finish my walk, I say, "Thank you."

Enjoy Mother Nature

If you love being in nature – on inter-urban trails, in parks, or the woods or forests, join with the beauty of the earth – trees, birds, squirrels, rabbits, flowers, ferns – see and observe everything with your sensual self.

- Smell it. What do you smell? Describe it – the earthy smell, the scent of pine, flowers, rotting leaves, decaying wood, the smell of rushing water, the smell of fresh air.

- Hear it. What do you hear? Children laughing, cars traveling, leaves rustling, water gurgling, the crushing of leaves underfoot, birds singing, branches swaying.

- Taste it. What do you taste? Are you chewing gum or drinking water? Taste the air, taste what you are smelling.

- See it. What do you see? Leaves on the bushes, their veins where they meet the branch, their colors, pine cones and needles on the fir trees, moss and lichens hanging off branches, fallen trees, the treetops reaching for the sky, the colors of the sky, the cloud formations, birds flying, chipmunks in the branches, people.

- Touch it. What do you feel? The soft breeze blowing on your face, the warm sun on your cheeks, cold air on your face and hands, your clothing touching your skin, raindrops, your hair moving in the wind, a leaf or branch brushing your skin.

How can you stimulate your hearing, seeing, smelling, tasting, and touching? Enjoy the little things that are magical, in the moment, and are true blessings. Use a lot of colorful adjectives, so the picture in your mind is beautifully and vividly imagined.

Plant some seeds and watch something grow. We are friends with each other. Treat all of nature with respect and caring.

The 5 A's and Reflection

Accept yourself first and give yourself the Attention you would give to another. Have compassion for yourself. Have Affection for yourself. Gently love yourself. Appreciate who you are. Allow yourself to be who you are no matter what. You may regret something or be upset about something you said, did, or thought. It is not worth wasting your good energy. Accept your decisions and try not to beat up on yourself or second guess yourself for those decisions. Take responsibility and ownership of them. Know you are freely choosing them, and you are choosing your attitude about your choices.

Let go of what you can't control. Your power belongs to you; keep it, cherish it, don't give it away to anyone else. Peace comes to you when you accept, surrender, and then let go with love in your heart. Periodically, stop, reflect, and listen to your heart; this is healthy for you to do.

Give yourself the gift of the 5As. Remind yourself that you are the most important person in your life. Pat yourself on the back. Congratulate yourself for every step you take. See how far you've come. Honor yourself along your journey. Remind yourself how deserving you are. You are perfect just the way you are, whole and complete. Your Story belongs to you; own it and love it.

Your Story belongs to you;
own it and love it.

Trust in the 3 Laws of the Universe (Abraham-Hicks)

Law of Attraction: That which is like unto itself is drawn.

Law of Deliberate Creation: That which you give thought to and that which you believe or allow or expect, is.

Law of Allowing: I am that which I am and I am willing to allow all others to be that which they are.

You are the creator of your life experiences. You get to choose what you want the world around you to be like. How you think creates your reality. If you are living a happy life right now, it's because of the happy thoughts you have about your life. If you are living an unhappy life right now, it's because of the unhappy thoughts you have about your life. You attract into your life what you are thinking about and the story you tell about your life. If you think, "I don't want to be in debt and broke all the time," debt and being broke is what you'll attract into your life. But if you think "I have plenty of money" that is what you'll attract into your life.

You attract into your life what you are thinking about and the story you tell about your life.

What you think and say now will be your future. If you're having health issues, instead of dwelling on the illness, focus your attention on the parts of your body that feel good and picture that goodness spreading throughout your body. Be grateful for the healthy parts, your positive attitude, and every breath you take. If you want fulfilling and happy relationships, see all people as good. Find something you like about others that's positive. Attract what you want. Pay attention to your thoughts, words, and actions. Are they what you want and desire? Are they what you don't want and desire? Are they deliberate? Are they automatic? Invite in the people and experiences you want to be a part of your life by including them with your thoughts.

Prepare your life right now for your future. Use your toolbox – think positive thoughts, take time to meditate and quiet your mind, focus on the good in your life and around you, do those things that make you smile and feel good, make a list of those things, make a vision or picture board, create affirmation cards, be grateful for what you have, and don't let life happen to you – create it, want it, desire it.

Use your toolbox. You are the primary tool; the most important, magnificent, and effective tool in your life. All you ever wanted and all you ever need is inside of you. You came into this world with it. You were created and born of Pure Love. Be who you are. Be the Real You and allow all others to be who they are.

"Be a good human being, a warm-hearted, affectionate person. That is my fundamental belief." -- Dalai Lama

---

Prayer

Quieting your mind in silence will connect you to the real you and Source, God, Universe, Divine Life, Creator. Call upon the power of God in you when you need support. You can rely on it. It is always available. All you have to do is ask. Ask for what you want. Ask for what you need. Ask for what to do. Then give thanks often. Prayer is a tool to use to build your spiritual, emotional, mental, and physical self.

We are One with all. Connecting as One through prayer brings the real you to a place of happiness and love. Peace and joy will envelop you when you stop the chatter in your head and let go of any limiting thoughts and focus on a stillness that soothes your soul. Stop and pray in stillness throughout your day, even for a minute or less. Ask for what you want. Silently or aloud, it will help clarify what that is. You will feel so renewed and connected for the rest of your day.

Some prayers you could use are:

"Source, God, Universe, Divine Life, Creator, what are you asking from me that I'm not getting? Help me to see what you want me to do."

"How can I best serve my soul?"

"Help me know the Real me so I can share myself with those around me."

"Source, God, Universe, Divine Life, Creator, how can I serve my highest good? "What can I do to make the world a better place?"

"Guide me to my highest good."

"My prayer is Thank You."

Ask and listen for the answer. Know that Source, God, Universe, Divine Life, Creator is Pure Love, and that's how your answer will come through your open heart. When you need to be held and loved, call on the Source to hold you, wrap energy around you, and bathe you in pure unconditional love.

Create your own prayers. They can be silent or out loud. Prayers come from inside of you and can be for anything or about anything, it's your choice, and it's all good. You can pray for:

- Gratitude and thankfulness
- Guidance and support when faced with a challenge or need strength
- What you want – abundance, strength, good health, relationships
- Forgiveness. – for yourself and others
- 5A's – Attention, Affection, Appreciation, Acceptance, Allowing

Mirror Work
(Louise Hay and Robert Holden)

Mirror work can help you become aware of the things you do and the words you say to yourself. Mirror work can help you let go of things that don't serve you and become more aware of the way you talk to yourself. It can help you listen to your words and turn them around to positive affirmations. It helps to quiet your inner critic and become your biggest fan.

As you wash your face or brush your teeth in the morning, look into the mirror at your reflection and look only into your eyes. You are not looking at your body, your hair, or your face. Look at the real you inside. Say out loud to the real you, "(Your name), I love you. Life loves you. What does your Soul need to know today? What does your Soul need to do today? What does your Soul need to say and to whom?" Whenever you pass a mirror throughout your day, say, "I love you (Your name)."

Louise Hay and Robert Holden offer a program on mirror work. Here is a sampling you can use. It's more effective if you create your own that means something to you. Then put them on notecards or sticky notes and stick them to your mirror:

One way life loves me today is _____.

I say YES, to today. Today I am willing to make this the best day of my life. Today I am willing to make this the happiest day of my life.

I am blessed

I follow my joy.

I prosper at every turn.

One thing I am truly grateful for in my life is

_____ .

Smiling and Laughter

Regardless of how you are feeling, a smile is something you have to give. Sometimes it may be the only thing. And sometimes it is enough. A smile is free.

Your smile creates goodness and welcomes those around you. It puts others at ease and makes them glad to be around you. It's uplifting for you at the same time. Your smile says, "Hey, join me in being happy and alive at this moment."

You will make someone's day and surely your own. What you give will come back to you.

"Breathing in, I calm body and mind.

Breathing out, I smile." A breathing meditation

by Buddhist monk Thich Nhất Hạnh

The world is your mirror.

The good you find in others is in you too.

*The faults you find in others
are your faults as well.*

*After all, to recognize something,
you must know it.*

*The possibilities you see in others
are possible for you as well.*

*The beauty you see around
you is your beauty.*

*The world around you is a reflection, a mirror showing
you the person you are.*

*To change your world,
you must change yourself.*

*To blame and complain
will only make matters worse.*

*Whatever you care about
is your responsibility.*

What you see in others shows you yourself.

*See the best in others,
and you will be your best.*

Give to others, and you give to yourself.

*Appreciate beauty,
and you will be beautiful.*

Admire creativity, and you will be creative.

Love, and you will be loved.

Seek to understand,
and you will be understood.
Listen, and your voice will be heard.
Teach and you will learn.
Show your best face to the mirror,
and you'll be happy
With the face looking back at you.

- Unknown

Find something to laugh about. Whether it's watching a comedy on television, or watching funny puppy or baby-laughing videos on your phone, a squirrel jumping through the branches of a tree, children playing, or watching an ant carry something, make faces in a mirror or with your phone apps. There are so many ways and places to look for something that will put a smile on your face or make you roar with laughter. Laughter is a way to help you heal by releasing stress and giving your immune system a boost. It makes your mind and physical body happy. Give it a try to brighten your day and maybe someone else's day by passing it on.

Journaling

Journaling is a tool that can help you cope with overwhelming emotions. If you need to define what you are feeling, express an emotion or thoughts, let go of stress, or find clarity, then write it down. Write down the things that make you happy, things that bring you pain, big things, little things, all the things you value and want to honor.

Journaling is a way to process what is going on. You can be alone, keep it private and do it by yourself. Find paper and pencil, a writing journal, or use your phone's notepad and just start writing, letting it flow. You don't need to edit your writing. You can date it and go back and reread it any time.

Whatever thoughts, feelings, or ideas pop into your head, write them down. The physical act of writing can be very healing.

One writing activity you might enjoy is **Positive Aspects About Me.**

Here are some ideas:

- I smile a lot and have a beautiful smile
- I am strong walker
- I have a pretty face and unique hazel eyes

- I have stamina
- I am a great teacher
- I acknowledge others by saying, "good morning," "hi," "how are you"
- I care about how others feel
- I have a healthy, strong, and beautiful body
- I'm fun to be around
- I have a good sense of humor
- I encourage others to be/do their best.
- I see positive aspects in others
- I help people see the good in themselves

EFT (Emotional Freedom Technique) or Tapping

Tapping works to rewire the brain to bring both the body and mind back into balance. By shifting your unconscious beliefs and emotions, you shift the chemicals being released into the body affecting your nervous system, your digestive and endocrine systems, your hormones, and your energy levels. It works similarly to acupuncture by focusing on energy points on the side of your hand (karate chop), eyebrow, side of the eye, under the eye, under the nose, the chin, collarbone, under the arm, and top of your head.

Tap lightly on these energy points while repeating phrases relating to your problem. You start a Tapping session by looking at the problem – what's bothering you at the time. It could be a physical pain like an ache in your lower back. It could be an emotional pain like resentment toward another person. It could be anything you want to look at and work through – poor sleep, stress, anxiety. It could be something you want more of in your life – peace, love, forgiveness. You address the negative aspects and then give yourself permission to feel the way you do before moving on to affirmations and what you want.

Nick Ortner (for one) offers a Tapping World Summit each year full of free activities, guidance, and training in this technique. He also has a website and a cellphone app. Here's a link on the basics of it and how to do it:

https://www.thetappingsolution.com/what-is-eft-tapping/

This is a way to release and free yourself from being stuck. You can use it for physical pain, forgiveness, fear, needing courage, releasing guilt, stress, self-doubt, health issues, releasing the past, life traumas, grief - every possibility that holds you back from being happy and living in your soul's joy can be addressed through Tapping.

Visualization

Visualization allows you to picture the future and lets your thoughts flow to that picture. You can mentally rehearse, practice, or picture anything you can imagine or dream. It only takes a few minutes. If you want to lose weight, if you want to change a habit, if you want to buy a new car, if you want a specific job, or if you want to be happy, visualize it like it's already happened.

Your mind does not know the difference between something you actually experienced or something you've vividly imagined. You can use your imagination to create anything you want in your life. If you picture the end result in your mind, you will find success. It's already there, the good is already there, and it will bring about the physical manifestation of it quicker.

Your mind does not know the difference between something you actually experienced or something you've vividly imagined. You can use your imagination to create anything you want in your life.

Athletes use their imagination all the time to improve their performance. Time is not a factor. Look around less and imagine more. What do you want to see? What do you want to have? What do you want to do? What new strengths, possibilities, and adventures do you want to experience? You can create joy in every moment. You can create the life of your dreams. You can create endlessly. Using your imagination can take you anywhere, everywhere. There are no limits. You can create beyond your current life. The possibilities are endless because you are endless. Use this tool to take you beyond your reality to where you want to go. Be there. Vividly see yourself living that life.

Start by quieting your thoughts and grounding yourself. You can do this sitting up or lying down, whichever is most comfortable for you. You can do this in any situation – while walking, at work, or at dinner.

Take a deep, deep breath that starts at your diaphragm, goes up through your chest, past your neck, and up to the top of your head, where you hold it for a long time, then release it slowly. Do that a few times before you begin to breathe normally and start visualizing what you choose to see. In a social setting, one deep breath is usually enough to get you centered. Start your visualization based on what you desire at the time. Deep, sincere, honest desire is the key to training your mind to support what your soul knows and wants. Focus on and desire a loving heart in all situations.

The stronger your desire is, the more your mind wants to go along with it.

If you need help with protecting yourself from someone's negativity, a self-defeating magazine ad, or TV spot, picture a clear film of self-love surrounding you that can't be penetrated by any negative thoughts, emotions, or advertisement. If you need support and love from Source, picture Angel wings wrapping themselves around you, holding you, and delivering to you what you need. If you need strength and courage to face someone, picture yourself twice the size of the person you're confronting and made of steel. Approach all situations with peace, love, and caring. Don't invite anger, fear, or resentment to join you; they can't penetrate your circle of self-love. See your pictures in detail. Everything from what you are wearing, who you are with, what your surroundings look like to the emotions you are feeling. The more vivid you make them, the more real they become.

Release Resistance

Resistance is your thoughts or beliefs that are not consistent with your desire, an underlying fear of what you really want. You resist when you feel vulnerable and then put up a shield of protection.

All suffering comes from believing our thoughts, feelings, and our fears, whether it's a fear of the unknown, death, loss, or change, to name a few. One of my fears is rejection. When I realized that is a part of my Story, my journey continued. Whether I live in fear or whether I embrace the moment and enjoy whatever comes my way is my choice. So I welcome in the feeling, accept it, and then, let it go.

All suffering comes from believing our thoughts, feelings, and our fears, whether it's a fear of the unknown, death, loss, or change, to name a few.

Start by letting the feeling be there without judging it; simply acknowledge and accept it as it is without trying to change it. See it as just a feeling. Then focus on letting out the energy behind it and releasing it. When you're feeling a negative emotion – sadness, heartache, loneliness, jealousy, anger, grief, fear, or are faced with a life change, check where in your body it is making itself known to you and where you really feel it. Sit with it and invite it to join you. Do not push it away. When you've had as much as you can take of it, release it and send it on its way.

Let go and accept things just as they are. Understand adversity is an opportunity for your well-being. Allow change to happen. Allow pain to happen; welcome in whatever comes. No resistance; allow. You can always revisit it again when you are able. Continue to revisit as needed. Eventually, the energy of the feeling will dissipate, and you will have released it and will feel lighter and at peace.

Release your anger, fears, pain, hurts, and old wounds. Release all of your past misbeliefs that aren't true. You've carried many since childhood, given to you by parents, teachers, friends, culture, and society. Some you've created on your own from television and social media. Release them by identifying them and letting them go. Now allow the good thoughts in.

Remember that you are a soul in human form and are a part of Source, God, Universe, Divine Life, Creator, and you are perfect just the way you are. Remember how loved you are. Remind yourself you want to be free of these thoughts and let them go. Ask Source to help you release each one you've identified and free yourself.

Step Outside of Yourself

When you are in situations where someone is pushing your buttons and upsetting you, stop and look within to listen to what is going on inside of you. Rather than blaming, reacting from emotion, comparing, competing, or judging, step back and become the observer. Try to remember the difference between judgment and observation. Take a deep breath and pay attention to your feelings and thoughts. Look at it all from a place of detachment and see all that is going on as a neutral observer. Can you see their sadness, pain, hurt, past trauma, guilt, or shame? What is calling out to you for love and attention? When you realize this, you can let go and release those feelings with the power of compassion and love. Love is your healer.

Remind yourself to separate a person's actions and behaviors from the person, as well as your own. You can be upset by a person's actions and behaviors and still love them for who they are. Allow others to be who they are, walk their own journey, and allow your real self to be the observer. Don't reject anyone, ever, for any reason. In so doing, you will learn to let go of your fear of rejection.

One day, try to just stop rejecting others and start accepting them as they are. Just let who they are or what they've done go. What you will notice is that you are giving yourself that very same thing: acceptance.

Do a Little Something Just for Yourself

What little something brings you joy?

Pick a wildflower every time you walk by one and put it somewhere on yourself – behind your ear, in your pocket, in a buttonhole, anywhere you can easily grab it and look at, smell, and totally enjoy its beauty, intricacy, and true magnificence of nature. Feel the breeze on your skin, smell the trees and touch the bark. Or maybe stop at the local park and skip or get on a swing and glide through the air feeling the movement throughout your body. Turn your favorite song on and dance with wild abandon. When your favorite song comes on the radio, sing along at the top of your lungs. Add hand, head, and body gestures to the act. You may enjoy a soak in the bathtub with your favorite oils and candlelight. Or maybe enjoy an ice cream cone, savoring each lick of your tongue as you swirl it around the creaminess. Find that higher level of physicality and aliveness that you knew as a child but slowly forgot as an adult.

Focus On Your Posture

Whether you are standing, moving, or sitting down, bring your shoulders to your ears and then slowly back down. Do this a few times to bring you back in the moment and release stress.

Keeping your back straight will help your breathing, digestion, as well as build your self-confidence, gives you energy and strength, and puts you in a good mood. Standing straight takes a load off your back, physically and mentally.

Childlike Play

Add play to your life as if experiencing life for the first time. No matter how old you are, the child in you is always with you. Be trusting and spontaneous. Get your entire body into it. You can be an airplane with your arms straight out from your sides, moving them up and down. If you live in a place where you get snow, make snow angels by lying in the snow on your back and with your arms at your side and legs together, then start flapping them up and down in the snow. When you get up and look at the impression in the snow, it looks like an angel.

On a clear night, lie down in the grass and look up at the stars, or during the day, look up at the clouds and let your imagination go. What do you see? Play in a pile of leaves or just kick them with your feet. Listen to the sound they make and the way they feel. Find a child's playground and get on a swing, climb a jungle gym or play on any of the toys. Yes, you may be a bit big for them, but they are fun.

Smell a flower and look closely at its petals or stare at the intricacies of a bug, the way it looks and moves. Paint, draw, mold some clay, eat with your fingers, play with a pet to add play to your life. You can even add play to your everyday tasks. Make a puzzle out of doing laundry or cooking. Make a game out of cleaning and vacuuming. Any activity can be interesting and fun if you turn it into play just by looking at life differently.

Try looking at your world, your environment like a child does. Watch children at play, their movements, their curiosity and innocence, and lack of fear. They will try anything without fear of how they look or what anyone else thinks. Listen to children at play. They are always laughing and giggling at every little thing. Even an insect can bring great joy. Children see the world with awe, purity, beauty, and wonder. Everything will look new and fresh. You can look at the world this way. So, add some play to your life. Be trusting, open, and spontaneous. What makes you get silly and laugh?

Go Outside and Play

"Go outside and play!" said God.

"I have given you Universes as fields to run free in!

And here — take this and wrap yourself in it —

It's called: LOVE

and It will always, always keep you warm.

And stars! The sun and the moon and the stars!

Look upon these often,

for they will remind you of your own light!

And eyes ... oh, gaze into the eyes of every Lover.

Gaze into the eyes of every ... every other

for they have given you their Universes

as fields to run free in.

There.

I have given you everything you need.

Now go, go, go outside

and

play!"

Home Remembers Me: Medicine Poems © 2007 Em Claire

Positive Attitude

Having a positive attitude is a choice. Whenever you're faced with a challenging situation that brings on negative thinking, try to find a positive in it and focus on that aspect. Turn the negative into a positive. See it as a blessing. Each blessing you take time to find makes this world a better place. It's a choice you can make for yourself. Your heart and your intuition will guide you to finding the equally true but happier thought about the very same situation. Lean into it. How you view it, happy or sad, good or bad, positive or negative, is completely up to you. Remember, we all have free will. Choose a positive attitude.

Having a positive attitude is a choice.

Brain Care

Our brain needs care just like the rest of our body. Get plenty of restful sleep (7-8 hours). Brains need healthy food with plenty of colors and particularly greens, fresh air, lots of water, exercise and movement, and positive outside input to nourish proper brain wave connections. Meditation can change the way your brain functions by stimulating different areas of the brain to improve your thinking.

Brains need care. Stimulate your five senses (sight, hearing, smell, taste, and touch), learn something new every day, even a small fact, solving puzzles, reading a book, or working on a computer. A pet can also provide new stimulation and companionship. Being around a pet opens you to thinking differently than you would with people. A pet isn't ego-driven, doesn't judge or compete, and doesn't try to control you or its environment. Pets can be uplifting to your spirit.

Social support, interaction with people, both in close relationships and with acquaintances, is necessary for the brain to thrive. Make connections with others wherever you go. If you find this difficult, start by making a list of people you care about and who care about you.

Make a decision to only allow uplifting energy in your life. Your brain waves, as a listener, will eventually connect with the speakers around you. Decide you only want to connect with positive energy. Consider how much negativity comes from the media – newspapers and television. You may want to consider your own reading material and listen to music, audiobooks, and podcasts.

Gradually distance yourself from people whose energy brings you down or requires you to heal after being around them. Have love in your heart for everyone, even those who are negative; send them love and step away. You can love them without including them in your life. Be open to people who are uplifting and a joy to be around. You can feed others in a positive way. Fill your life with people, spaces, and things that bring you joy. Joy is your birthright; you don't have to earn it. It's a choice to feel it and live it, and your brain will appreciate it.

Touch

Be a toucher. Better yet, be a hugger. Share your touches with every living thing. Caress the bark of a tree, touch its branches and leaves and send it love. Scratch a pet. Run your hand through its fur and give it a gentle massage. Give hugs to people, children, and adults. If that's not comfortable, put your hand on theirs, squeeze their shoulder or knee, or reach out with a caring handshake.

Practice Patience

Patience is trusting life. Trusting that you are exactly where you are supposed to be at every moment. Trusting that everything always works out and you cannot make a mistake when you let your inner wisdom guide you.

It's never too late to open yourself up to living a life of happiness, love, and joy. There is no time limit. There is no age limit. When you are ready, you will awaken, and you will move. Just be patient and gentle with yourself.

Patience will open your heart to receiving love and allows you to be a giver of love to everyone and everything. Slow your life down. Take deep breaths, meditate, walk in nature, journal, draw as you catch yourself when you begin to get overwhelmed with emotion. Patience allows you to accept and release.

Practice Loving Kindness and Compassion

We were all born good. We all have goodness inside of us. Remember this for yourself and others. Love yourself from the inside out. Love all living things. Love isn't just for a mate, friends, family members, or a pet. Love is from the inside out and is for all. Practice being loving to everyone and everything. As you remember the goodness, send out loving thoughts. When you practice out of love, then love will come back to you, a Circle of Love. Practice loving without conditions. Practice love every moment. We come from Pure Love; it's our birthright. It's who I am, and it's who you are.

Hold space for others by listening to them. Sometimes the greatest way to say something is by saying nothing at all (*Say Something* by Justin Timberlake). Send them positive energy and love instead of offering them advice, a solution, trying to fix them, correcting them, or robbing them of their pride and opportunity to learn. Each of us has our own journey, our own Story we must live in order to learn what we came into this world to learn.

Be kind to others, whether they are friends, acquaintances, or strangers. Let someone know you see and acknowledge them. Give them love and compassion, show them appreciation, accept them for who they are, and allow them to be. This can be done on the phone, on a computer, or face to face. The most effective act of kindness is to be happy, compassionate, and loving. Your behavior is the message to pass on to others.

The most effective act of kindness is to be
happy, compassionate, and loving.

Sharing of Yourself

Do more for others, selfless acts of kindness. When you give of yourself, your time, your energy, your space, it just plain feels good, and we all want to feel good.

Listen to people. They need to be heard. They want to talk about themselves. It makes them feel good, just like it makes you feel good when you talk about yourself. Spread happiness to others with the gift of your attention. Give by example to others: be loving, cooperate, help, care, be kind, be honest, be real.

When you give of yourself, give to yourself. Follow the Golden Rule: Do unto others as you would have it done unto you. It feels good to be a giver but don't get depleted; be mindful of your own energy and needs.

Think about an act of kindness that someone extended to you. How did it make you feel? You can start with one small act of kindness every day. It doesn't have to be big. You could open a door for someone. You could listen when someone needs to talk, not trying to solve anything or offer advice, simply giving someone your time and attention. Let someone know that you appreciate them by thanking them for something they have done for you. Say "I love you" to someone because they are important to you, and you are grateful they are in your life. Accept a stranger without judging their appearance, shortcomings, or mistakes.

You can make yourself available when someone needs help with yard work, running errands, or house cleaning. You can give time, clothing, or money to charity. Try silently blessing people, sending positive energy and good thoughts to all. Greeting all you meet with a smile, a wave, or kind remark. Each act of kindness will bring you as much joy as the recipient.

Another way you can pass the goodness on is by centering yourself in love by quieting your mind and relaxing your body. Then imagine Source, God, Universe, Divine Life, Creator filling you up with light. See this light glowing from you and wrapping itself around each person. Hold them in your light and love. From them, see it spreading out beyond as they continue to pass this goodness on.

There is a difference between helping others and doing for others what they need to do for themselves. Be careful with your help. If you help too much, you could actually hurt someone by making them dependent on you. It's hard to watch a person struggle with their life; you want to help them and make it easier for them. Sometimes you just want to do it for them. Instead, be a good example to them and allow them to live their own Story and develop their own skills so they will learn the lessons they came here to learn and receive the gifts they were meant to receive.

We all want to be a good person and grow, but we want to do it in our own way and in our own time. You can't make someone do something they aren't ready to do. You can't make someone love themselves and feel worthy any more than you can make someone stop feeling guilty or angry. What you can do, in your own way, is model positive behaviors and beliefs with love, faith, and hope in your heart.

Seek Support When Needed

How do you know it's time to seek help? If you are stuck, if you have recurring negative thoughts, if you no longer want to participate in things you used to enjoy, if you feel apathetic toward life, if you abuse drugs, alcohol, food, or anything just to cope, if you withdraw from life or if someone has noticed a concerning change in you, if you have tried to help yourself and nothing has worked, then it's time to seek help outside of yourself.

Seeking support will give you a clearer perspective and assist you in opening up to a positive change or movement. Talk to a friend. Bounce it off of someone you trust who is willing to listen. Listen to your favorite self-help authors, spiritualists, and philosophers (Hay House Publishing has many). Join a support group. Talk to a counselor, coach, therapist, or guide. Even though everyone around us may feel we do not have problems or anything to worry about, we can all use help on occasion, and we should not be afraid to seek it out.

YOUR OWN TOOLBOX

Build yourself a Toolbox that you create by choosing your own tools, those you will practice using every day that will help you use the gifts you were born with. Know that you are a tool also, the key tool that drives you. You are Pure Positive Energy, you are Pure Love, and that means you have happiness and joy already inside of you. Everything you desire is within you. Nurture it; nurture yourself from the inside out. You are the only one who can do this for you. Your tools will help you.

Everything you desire is within you. Nurture it; nurture yourself from the inside out. You are the only one who can do this for you.

CONCLUSION

"Who Am I?"

"Am I a human being?"

"Am I a soul?"

"Why am I here? Why was I born?"

"What's my purpose? What did I come into this world to do?"

Who Am I? – "I am a spiritual being, pure awareness, a soul, the Real Mary. I Am more than my body, my mind, or what I do and say. I Am One with You and Source and I came from Pure Love."

Why Am I here? – "I Am here to learn, evolve, experience, and create, to grow as a soul. I Am here as One with all things, and I am part of Source, God, Universe, Divine Life, Creator, and so is everything."

What is my purpose? – "My purpose is to be happy and live a human life filled with love and joy. I am here to remember who I Am. I Am here to pass this love and happiness on to all things; I am here to be Love. I am here to learn and be of service to humanity by being who I really Am, the soul, the Real

Mary. I Am here to accomplish my spiritual purpose while, at the same time, living a human life."

The answers to my questions, the mysteries of life, were inside of me all along. It's already in you and has always been and will always be in you. It was my choice to open up and seek them. I didn't need to click any ruby slippers to be happy and filled with love. You can do the same whenever you are ready and desire to. I was always seeking a solution and/or a distraction to the problems in my life, my lack of purpose, my loneliness, the answer to "why am I here?" When I realized I had the answers all along, I needed to quietly look inside, let go, release, and surrender.

Letting go of the superficial, the artificial, the pretending, need for approval, judging, putting my ego to work with the real me, and allowing myself to be vulnerable, is humbling. When I decided that other people's and society's expectations weren't mine and I was in charge of my life, love, and happiness, I stopped seeking and began living. If I can do it, you can do it.

How would you answer these questions now? Would your answers be the same or different from when you started reading this book?

I ask that you sit with these ideas I've shared. Do they feel comfortable to you? Do they mesh with your sense of yourself? Do they fit with your experiences in life? Do they ring true to your inner being? If you answer yes to any of these questions, then you are on your way to opening up to happiness, joy, and the love already inside of you.

As you continue to live your Story, live it happily, live it magically, live it uplifting and filled with love and joy. As you grow in love, joy, and peace, pass the goodness on by looking for opportunities to share it with others. The most effective way you can help anyone with anything is by being the goodness. Your example can help people help themselves. So, be the goodness to everyone and everything all the time. Your Story can be a messenger of hope.

How would you know light if you didn't know darkness, how would you know life if you didn't know death, how would you know happiness and joy if you didn't know sadness, how would you know love if you didn't experience fear? Each is part of the other. It's all part of the same thing, part of the same energy, part of a Circle. It is all One. We are all One because we are part of the same energy, Source, God, Universe, Divine Life, Creator, as are all thoughts, emotions, and living and non-living beings. We are all One, there is no separation. As One, we all have a Story, and we are all part of a Circle. Your Story continues on eternally. There is no end. Your Story is a Circle.

We are all One because we are part of the same energy, Source, God, Universe, Divine Life, Creator, as are all thoughts, emotions, and living and non-living beings. We are all One, there is no separation. As One, we all have a Story, and we are all part of a Circle. Your Story continues on eternally. There is no end. Your Story is a Circle.

ABOUT MARY K. HILD

Mary K. Hild considers herself a messenger of inspiration, motivation, and encouragement.

With more than two decades as a counselor in both alternative and traditional schools, Mary has positively impacted the lives of hundreds of students (many of whom she is still in contact with).

Her experience teaching Special Education and many years of substitute teaching at the high school level developed her compassion and sharpened her wit.

Mary's understanding of humanity broadened during her 14 years in the Air Force Reserves, where she traveled through much of Europe and Asia.

Born and raised in Northern Minnesota, she has lived most of her adult life in Washington state's beautiful Puget Sound region.

Mary divides her time between Federal Way, WA, with her husband of 41 years and her Ocean Shores getaway. Whether she's partying or listening to music, reading or meditating, hiking in the mountains, or walking her dog, Ginger, on the beach, Mary loves to be in nature!

Wherever she is, she meets people and connects with them. Mary K. Hild is a true lover of life!